WOODWORKING PROJECTS

60 Easy-to-Make Projects from HANDS ON Magazine

A Shopsmith®/Rodale Press Publication

Shopsmith®, Inc.
6640 Poe Avenue
Dayton, Ohio 45414

Rodale Press, Inc.
33 East Minor Street
Emmaus, Pennsylvania 18049

RODALE

Preface

This book contains sixty woodworking project plans from back issues of *HANDS ON*, The Home Workshop Magazine published by Shopsmith, Inc. These easy-to-make wooden projects are sure to provide any woodworker, from beginner to expert, with hours of fun and enjoyment in the shop. Many of the projects are ideal gifts for friends or family, and they're suitable for most any occasion—Christmas, birthdays, weddings, etc.

These projects were designed to be completed in a short amount of time using the Shopsmith Mark V and accessories; however, most of the projects can be built using a variety of hand and power tools. An overarm pin router is required to build several of the projects, and these are designated with the symbol RA . Special woodworking techniques have been referred to in *Power Tool Woodworking for Everyone* by R.J. De-Cristoforo, Reston Publishing Company.

Many thanks go out to *HANDS ON* readers who have contributed their project ideas to the magazine over the years. Over a third of the projects in this book were contributed by these readers, and their projects have provided hours of enjoyment for other woodworkers.

A final note: As with all woodworking endeavors, always keep safety your top priority. And before starting any of the projects in this book (or any woodworking project for that matter), be sure to read through the entire plan first before making any cuts.

Library of Congress Cataloging in Publication Data
Main entry under title:

Woodworking projects.

Includes index.
1. Woodwork.   I. Shopsmith, Inc.   II. Hands on!
TT180.W68   1984   684'.08   84–22194
ISBN 0-87857-618-5   hardcover
ISBN 0-87857-615-0 (previously ISBN 0-937558-12-5)   paperback

© Copyright 1984 by
Shopsmith®, Inc.
6640 Poe Avenue
Dayton, Ohio 45414-2591

Printed in the United States of America.

Rodale Press Edition

1986
10 9 8 7 6 5 4 3   Hardcover
10 9 8 7 6 5   Paperback

Publisher: Shopsmith®, Inc./Rodale Press, Inc.
Design: Kearns Design Studio
Text Preparation: Scharff Associates, Ltd.
Cover Photography: Dan Gabriel

Contents

Accessories

Because wood has a natural beauty all its own, items made from wood enhance any room in any home. Woodworking projects take on even more meaning when a project is combined with a particular function, such as candle sconces that add to the decor or a chess set that provides entertainment. In this section there are over fifteen projects that are sure to bring delight to any woodworker...and provide enjoyment for the entire family.

THE QUICKEST WAY TO MAKE GIFTS THAT PLEASE

From *HANDS ON* Nov/Dec 82

by Paul Lucas

"Ahh! Done—and with time to spare! This year's Christmas presents were a pleasure, especially since I was able to get them done early."

These were my thoughts one evening last year as I paused to turn out my shop lights. Knowing I was an amateur woodworker, each of my four aunts had wanted me to make her something out of wood.

All of my aunts are great letter writers, so I decided on a useful gift—a letter box for each aunt. Now the gifts sat in a neat row on my workbench—finished with lots of time to spare before they were to be wrapped in colorful Christmas paper.

It wasn't always this way. I used to find myself scurrying to finish my presents during those last few hours of Christmas Eve!

But throughout the years, I've discovered a few secrets. I know that gift making can be even more enjoyable if you realize one important fact—it's easier and quicker to make duplicates of a gift than it is to make several different ones.

In my small shop, I find that in addition to my woodworking tools, there are actually six techniques I use that save me time, money and make my woodworking easier.

Before making duplicate gifts, there are a couple of ground rules I follow. First, I try to keep my shop organized and uncluttered. Tools, fasteners, glue, and other shop items should all be stored in their proper place. I spend my time *using* the tools, not looking for them. Be-

sides being safer, a neatly arranged shop allows me to do woodworking, rather than tool-searching.

After I've decided on my project, I make a master pattern. I take time to measure precisely and cut carefully, but I only do this step once. Making one master pattern eliminates the time-consuming steps of laying out and measuring each piece separately.

When I'm making duplicate gifts, I don't make each one individually from start to finish. Rather, I cut the parts for all gifts at the same time using the same setup and proceed in sequence. For example, I bandsaw all the pieces for the gifts at the same time. Then, I sand all the pieces, and so on. Cutting down on my setup time actually gives me more productive hours in the shop. By completing one operation for all the pieces during the same setup, I can easily make the parts to all the gifts in just a little more time than it takes me to make one.

So far, I've laid the groundwork, but what are those other secrets I use? The ones I've chosen to discuss with you here have been most helpful when making duplicate gift projects.

Most of my projects require stock less than 3/4" thick. When I need thin stock, I resaw my lumber. Resawing is a bandsaw operation that makes thin boards out of thick ones (see *Power Tool Woodworking for Everyone*). If you resaw wide boards (4" to 6"), use a wide miter gauge extension.

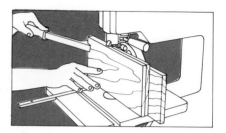

When resawing, use a miter gauge extension and remember it must be parallel to the 1/2" blade. Always use a push stick for the last few inches of the cut.

Resawing also saves me money. Creating two pieces of 5/16" stock from a 3/4" thick board gives me twice the lumber to duplicate pieces. I get two pieces of usable lumber for the price of one.

Pad sawing is another technique that increases my productivity. I stack two or more boards on top of each other. I then tape them together using masking or double-faced carpet tape. After I trace the pattern on the top board, I bandsaw all the taped pieces at once (see *Power Tool Woodworking for Everyone*). I make my cut slightly outside the pattern line so I can sand the pieces to their finished dimension. Pad sawing is much faster than bandsawing each piece separately.

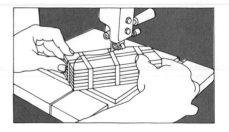

Stack several pieces of thin stock and tape them together. Then, pad saw them as one board.

Several of my small projects call for cutting tapers. To do this I use a fixed taper jig.

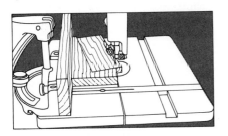

Using a taper jig, you can cut duplicate tapers without measuring each board.

This jig has one straight side for riding the rip fence and a slanted side with a heel to gauge the taper. By using this jig, I can duplicate the tapers accurately from one piece to another without measuring each piece (see *Power Tool Woodworking for Everyone*).

Belt and disc sanders are great for sanding flat surfaces or corners, but what about concave curves? My answer is to use the drum sander. But freehand drum sanding does not give me the accuracy I need. My drum sanding jig gives me this accuracy when I sand curves. The drum sanding jig works on the pin routing principle. The pin is the same diameter as the sanding drum and slightly less than my master pattern.

First, I tape the sawed workpiece to my pattern, using double-faced carpet tape. Then, I place the pattern against the drum sanding pin. The template (my pattern) rides on the drum sanding pin while the rotating drum removes exactly the correct amount of stock. Result? An exact duplicate of the pattern.

Use the drum sanding jig along with your master pattern to accurately sand curves.

Besides cutting and sanding, drilling is another operation that can be streamlined. When I need to drill a hole in exactly the same place in several pieces, I use a stop block. The stop block can be used on the fence in either the drill press or horizontal boring mode. (See *Power Tool Woodworking for Everyone*.) Using the stop block is more convenient than a C-clamp and a piece of scrap wood. This stop block rides on the fence. When properly positioned, this jig stops the workpiece. Hold the workpiece firmly against the stop block, table, and fence while drilling. Since the workpiece is stopped in exactly the same position each time, the holes are drilled in exactly the same position.

The stop block eliminates the need for you to mark each hole separately before you drill.

By using the pad sawing technique, it is possible to pad drill. Stack several workpieces on the table and against the fence; then, drill through all of them at once. Always use a backup board to avoid drilling into the fence.

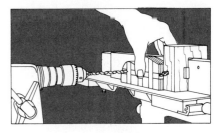

Apply the pad sawing technique to drilling so that you can pad drill.

Finally, an invaluable aid to my small shop is a router arm. I use it a lot. Pin routing eliminates tedious and time-consuming repetitive work. It takes time to make the required template, but once it is made, I can rout two or two thousand pieces—each an exact duplicate of the first.

By using these jigs and techniques, my gift making and gift giving are a real pleasure. Try these secrets the next time your aunts would like you to "make them something out of wood." You, too, will be smiling the night before Christmas.

LETTER BOX

From *HANDS ON* Nov/Dec 82

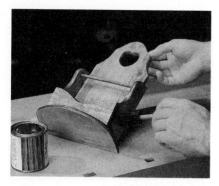

Here's a handy gift you can easily make for the holidays. Construct one or more using the techniques we discussed on pages 6-7. Hang the finished product on the wall or set it on a desk to hold all important mail.

1. Resaw stock to 5/16" thick. Sand or plane the sawn surfaces smooth.
2. Cut stock to size according to the List of Materials.
3. Cut out the heart shape in the back (A) with a router arm or a jigsaw.
4. Cut the side tapers using the fixed taper jig (see page 7).
5. Cut out all other parts on the bandsaw. Use the pad sawing technique (see page 6) to cut the curves.
6. Drill holes in the sides (B) using a stop block and the pad drilling technique (see page 7).
7. Assemble all pieces with yellow woodworker's glue and small brads. Insert dowel into sides (B) before attaching sides to back (A). Sand the project, and apply the finish of your choice.

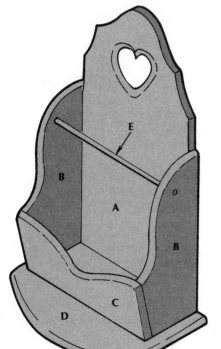

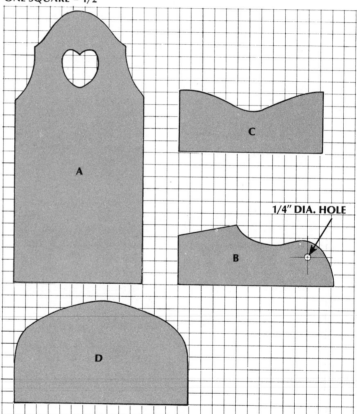

ONE SQUARE = 1/2"

1/4" DIA. HOLE

LIST OF MATERIALS

(finished dimensions in inches)

A	Back	5/16 × 5-1/2 × 11-1/4
B	Sides (2)	5/16 × 2-1/2 × 6-5/8
C	Front	5/16 × 2-1/2 × 6-1/8
D	Bottom	5/16 × 4-1/4 × 7-3/8
E	Dowel	1/4 dia. × 6-1/8

LANTERN HOLDER

From *HANDS ON* Nov/Dec 81

The age-old lantern, complete with lantern holder, still casts a warm, friendly light in the most modern home. The notched shelf of the holder cradles the lantern and the mirror reflects the lantern's soft glow throughout the room.

To construct the holder use a jigsaw, bandsaw, or pin router. Pin routing is a great way to make more than one holder, and here's how to do it.

1. Make two pin routing fixtures: one to rout out the shelf (B) and the back (A) with its design and dado, and the other to rout out the mirror recess in the back.

2. Set up for pin routing with a 1/4" pin and straight router bit.

3. Attach stock to the shelf/back fixture, and rout the outside contour, dado, and the inside design of the shelf (B) and back (A). Set the shelf aside.

4. Attach the back stock to the mirror recess fixture, and rout a 3/16" deep area in the back to hold the mirror.

5. Round the back and shelf edges with a 3/8" piloted rounding-over bit (with no pin). Note that edges near dado joint aren't rounded.

6. Glue the shelf (B) to the back (A) and reinforce the joint with #12 × 1-1/2" flathead wood screws.

7. Fasten the mirror in the back with push points or tiny wire brads.

Try some variations with the lantern holder—a different design in the back or even a solid back. You may substitute stained glass for the mirror. Or, even build a solid shelf to hold candles or potted plants.

LIST OF MATERIALS

(finished dimensions in inches)

A	Back	3/4 × 7 × 21-3/4
B	Shelf	3/4 × 7 × 7-1/4

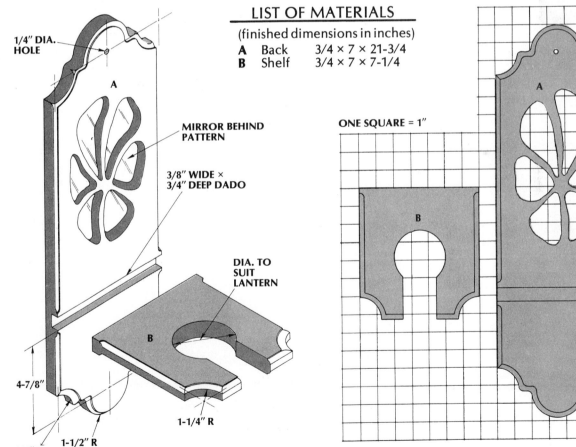

1/4" DIA. HOLE

A

MIRROR BEHIND PATTERN

3/8" WIDE × 3/4" DEEP DADO

DIA. TO SUIT LANTERN

B

4-7/8"

1-1/4" R

1-1/2" R

1-1/4" R

1-1/4" R

ONE SQUARE = 1"

A

B

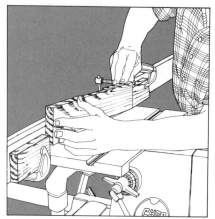

Organize yourself with this attractive, compact work chest. Use it to store tools, silverware, or hobby supplies. You can make fewer, deeper drawers or add more smaller drawers. Cleverly hidden dadoes and rabbets strengthen this project.

1. Cut joinery with dado blades and two stop blocks clamped to the rip fence, one block to help you start the cut and the other to end it.

2. Lower the workpiece over the dado blades *slowly;* then, feed it against the rotation of the blades. Turn off the machine before removing the workpiece from the table.

3. Dry-clamp the cabinet sides (A), and top and bottom (B).

4. Space the drawer guides (P) inside the cabinet. Check this spacing with the drawer sides (G, H, J) and temporarily tack the guides in position.

5. Adjust the table so the kerfs for the fingerholds in the drawer fronts (D, E, F) are one-third the height of the drawer fronts.

6. Glue the drawers together and check their fit in the cabinet. Adjust the guides (P), if necessary.

7. Attach the guides (P) to the cabinet sides (A) with countersunk screws. Pull out the temporary nails.

8. Glue the entire cabinet together and slide in the drawers.

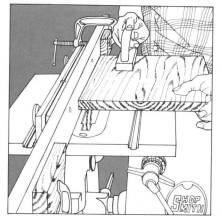

Control the stop dadoes by using an auxiliary fence with stop blocks clamped at the front and back.

Lower drawer front between the stop blocks.

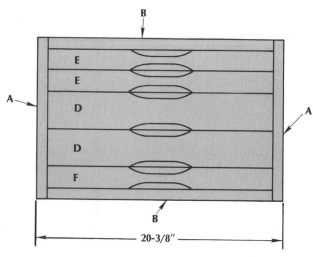

DRAWER POSITION LAYOUT

LIST OF MATERIALS

(finished dimensions in inches)

A	Cabinet sides (2)	3/4 × 9-3/4 × 13
B	Cabinet top & bottom (2)	3/4 × 9-3/4 × 19-5/8
C	Cabinet back	3/4 × 12-1/4 × 19-5/8
D	Drawer fronts (2)	3/4 × 3 × 18-3/4
E	Drawer fronts (2)	3/4 × 1-3/4 × 18-3/4
F	Drawer front	3/4 × 1-1/2 × 18-3/4
G	Drawer sides (4)	3/4 × 3 × 8-1/2
H	Drawer sides (4)*	3/4 × 1-3/4 × 8-1/2
J	Drawer sides (2)*	3/4 × 1-1/2 × 8-1/2
K	Drawer backs (2)	3/8 × 3 × 18
L	Drawer backs (2)*	3/8 × 1-3/4 × 18
M	Drawer back*	3/8 × 1-1/2 × 18
N	Drawer bottoms (5)	1/8 × 7-5/8 × 17-1/2
P	Drawer guides (10)	1/2 × 1/2 × 7-3/8

*Not shown.

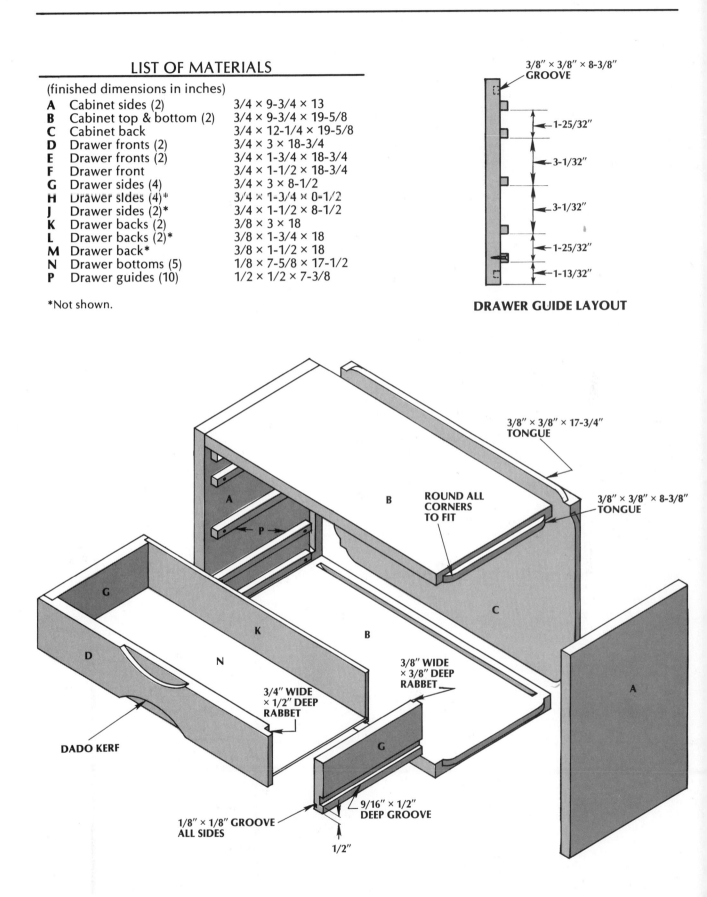

3/8″ × 3/8″ × 8-3/8″
GROOVE

1-25/32″

3-1/32″

3-1/32″

1-25/32″

1-13/32″

DRAWER GUIDE LAYOUT

3/8″ × 3/8″ × 17-3/4″
TONGUE

ROUND ALL
CORNERS
TO FIT

3/8″ × 3/8″ × 8-3/8″
TONGUE

3/8″ WIDE
× 3/8″ DEEP
RABBET

3/4″ WIDE
× 1/2″ DEEP
RABBET

DADO KERF

1/8″ × 1/8″ GROOVE
ALL SIDES

9/16″ × 1/2″
DEEP GROOVE

1/2″

11

GUMBALL MACHINE

From *HANDS ON* Sept/Oct 80

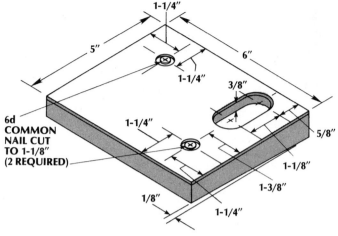

BASE FIXTURE

This ingenious toy will fascinate children and adults. A concealed spiral groove allows the gumball to travel around the delivery shaft and into a shallow pocket to be picked up. Here's how to make one using an overarm pin router.

1. Make two fixtures—one to rout out the recess in the base and the other to aid in routing the spiral groove in the delivery shaft.

The base fixture is made from a piece of sink cutout 5″ wide × 6″ long. Cut out a 3/8″ thick plywood template, following our pattern, and nail the template to the particleboard side of the sink cutout. Use a 3/8″ table pin and a 3/8″ carbide-tipped straight router bit and rout the recess in the plastic laminated side of the sink cutout. Drill two 3/32″ diameter holes through the fixture for 6d nails to mount the base to the fixture. Countersink the nail heads. Use a bandsaw and taper the particleboard side of the fixture 1/8″ descending from the recess. Sand smooth.

The other fixture is made from a 1′ long 2 × 4. Cut a V-groove, 3/4″ deep, the length of the 2 × 4 using a table saw. Attach a 3/4″ × 1-1/4″ × 30″ strip to the 2 × 4 to clamp the fixture in place when routing the spiral groove.

2. Cut all pieces to size according to the List of Materials except the delivery shaft (D).

3. Drill holes in center block (A).
4. Insert 1″ dowel rod in center block and mark delivery hole and spiral groove.
5. Rout the spiral groove in the delivery shaft with a 1/4″ straight bit and V-block fixture.
6. Cut delivery shaft to length and chamfer end.
7. Insert delivery shaft in center block and drill delivery hole.
8. Attach base to base fixture and rout out the pocket using a 1/2″ table pin and a 1/2″ core box bit.
9. Remove base from fixture and cut chamfer around edges of base.
10. Finish all pieces.
11. Wax delivery shaft (D) and insert the delivery shaft and guide pin (C) in the center block (A). Do not glue.
12. Assemble remaining pieces.

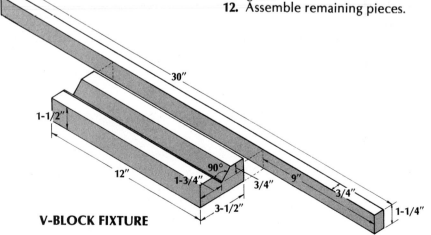

V-BLOCK FIXTURE

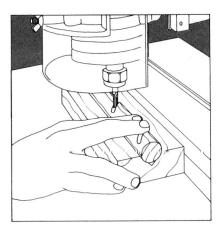

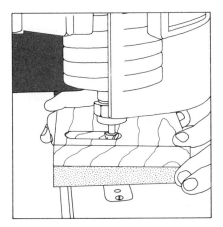

Route spiral groove in delivery shaft.
Use entire 36" dowel rod for safety.

Route pocket in base using fixture.

3/16" × 45° CHAMFER

1" DIA. HOLE

3/4" DIA. × 5/8" DEEP HOLE

1/4" DIA. × 1/4" DEEP HOLE

3-1/2"

1-3/4"

A

5/8"

1-1/2"

1"

1-5/8"

1/4"

1/8" SAW KERF CUT BEFORE DRILLING HOLES

3-1/4"

3-5/8"

CENTER BLOCK DETAIL

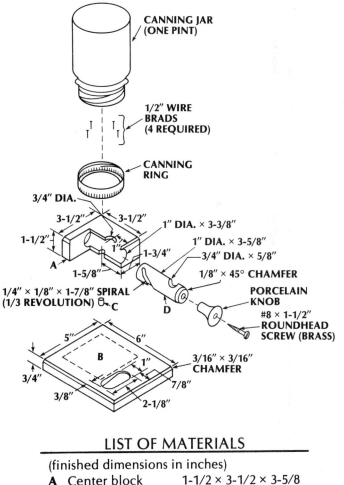

CANNING JAR (ONE PINT)

1/2" WIRE BRADS (4 REQUIRED)

CANNING RING

3/4" DIA.

3-1/2"

3-1/2"

1-1/2"

1"

1-3/4"

1" DIA. × 3-3/8"

1" DIA. × 3-5/8"

3/4" DIA. × 5/8"

1/8" × 45° CHAMFER

A

1-5/8"

1/4" × 1/8" × 1-7/8" SPIRAL (1/3 REVOLUTION) C

D

PORCELAIN KNOB

#8 × 1-1/2" ROUNDHEAD SCREW (BRASS)

5"

6"

B

1"

3/16" × 3/16" CHAMFER

3/4"

3/8"

7/8"

2-1/8"

3/4" DIA. × 5/8" DEEP

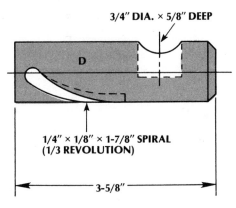

D

1/4" × 1/8" × 1-7/8" SPIRAL (1/3 REVOLUTION)

3-5/8"

DELIVERY SHAFT DETAIL

LIST OF MATERIALS

(finished dimensions in inches)

A	Center block	1-1/2 × 3-1/2 × 3-5/8
B	Base	3/4 × 5 × 6
C	Guide pin	1/4 dia. × 3/8
D	Delivery shaft	1 dia. × 3-5/8*

*Use entire 36" length of dowel when routing spiral groove.

PENCIL HOLDER

From *HANDS ON* Nov/Dec 83

Whether used for pencils and odds-and-ends to better organize a desktop or in the kitchen for holding utensils, this holder makes a great practical gift.

1. Start the project by gluing up a 3″ × 8″ × 5″ block of maple or a hardwood of your choice. You could even use a mixture of woods to create a colorful and unusual effect.

2. Square the glued-up stock, and transfer the pattern to it.

3. Mark the hole locations and drill the holes. Use Forstner bits since these leave a flat-bottomed hole.

4. Bevel the top on the table saw or bandsaw; then, cut out the contour on the bandsaw.

5. Sand the holder using the disc and drum sanders or the belt sander. Apply the finish of your choice.

ONE SQUARE = 1/2″

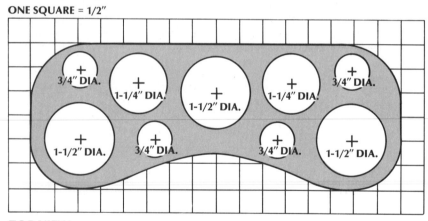

TOP VIEW

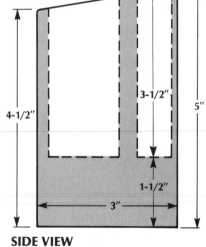

SIDE VIEW

DESKTOP BOOKSHELF

From *HANDS ON* Mar/Apr 82

Keep reference books handy with this simple-to-build, adjustable book rack. It's a sturdy, useful organizer for desktop, kitchen counter, or workbench.

1. Cut all pieces to size according to the List of Materials, roughing out the curves on the bandsaw or jigsaw. Curves can be readily sanded with the 2-1/4" and 1-1/2" drum sanders. If you want to make more than one, use the pad sawing technique (see page 6).

2. Glue and clamp the stretchers (A) to the spacers (B). Then, glue and clamp the feet (C) onto the ends of this assembly.

3. Sand the top and ends with the disc or belt sander.

4. Insert the adjustable ends (D). Glue the braces (E) into place. Allow about 1/32" clearance on each side for easy operation. Stain and seal with the finish of your choice.

LIST OF MATERIALS

(finished dimensions in inches)

A	Stretchers (2)	3/4 × 3 × 18
B	Spacers (2)	3/4 × 3/4 × 2
C	Feet (2)	3/4 × 1-1/2 × 10-1/2
D	Ends (2)	3/4 × 5 × 6-1/2
E	Braces (2)	3/4 × 3/4 × 4

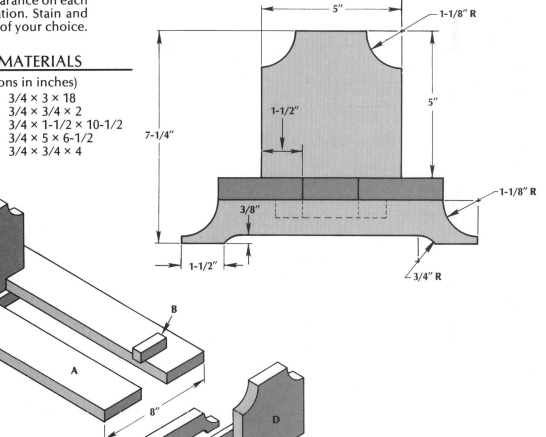

2" LONG × 3/8" DEEP DADO

BIRD FEEDER

From *HANDS ON* July/Aug 82

You'll take great pleasure in watching birds enjoy four-course meals from the separate food compartments which are unique to this feeder.

1. Select stock and materials. The front and back windows (J) and dividers (K) are plexiglass.

2. Cut all stock (except G) to size according to List of Materials, using the table saw.

3. Cut bevels. Tilt table 45° and cut bevels on deflectors (C). Tilt table 30° and cut bevels on the roof support (E). To cut the weather cap (G), tilt table 30° and cut V-groove on edge of wide board. Move the rip fence in 1/2" toward blade and repeat process to cut cap from wide stock.

4. Tilt table 7°; cut shingles (F).

5. Layout and cut contours on the ends (A, B) and dividers (K, L) with the bandsaw.

6. Rout grooves and rabbets, using a handheld router. Drill the 1/2" × 3/8" deep holes for the perches (H).

7. Nail the deflectors (C) together and attach them to the bottom (D) with brass brads.

8. Assemble the lower ends (A), front and back windows (J), and the bottom assembly with #8 × 1-1/4" brass flathead wood screws (do not insert perches until later). Assemble the upper ends (B) and the roof support (E) in the same manner and set them aside.

9. Fasten the compartment dividers (K) to the windows (J) with #4 × 1/2" brass roundhead wood screws.

10. Attach the six feed dividers (L) to the windows in the same manner. Attach the edging (M) to each side.

11. Remove one of the lower ends (A) and insert the two perches (H) and reassemble.

12. Fasten the shingles (F) to the feeder with brass brads.

13. Tack cap (G) in place and attach window sash locks to the ends (A, B).

LIST OF MATERIALS

(finished dimensions in inches)

A	Lower ends (2)	3/4 × 10-7/8 × 20-1/2
B	Upper ends (2)	3/4 × 7-1/4 × 12
C	Deflectors (2)	3/4 × 3-7/8 × 22
D	Bottom	3/4 × 10-1/2 × 22
E	Roof support	3/4 × 2-1/2 × 22
F	Shingles (18)	3/8 × 2-1/8 × 27-1/2
G	Weather cap	1/2 × 3/4 × 27-1/2
H	Perches (2)	1/2 dia. × 22-3/4
J	Windows (2)	1/4 × 7-1/2 × 22-1/2
K	Compartment dividers (3)	1/4 × 10-1/8 × 10-3/4
L	Feed dividers (6)	1/4 × 1-7/8 × 2-3/4
M	Edging (2)	1/4 × 1-1/2 × 22

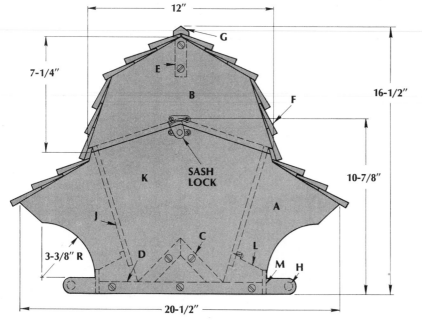

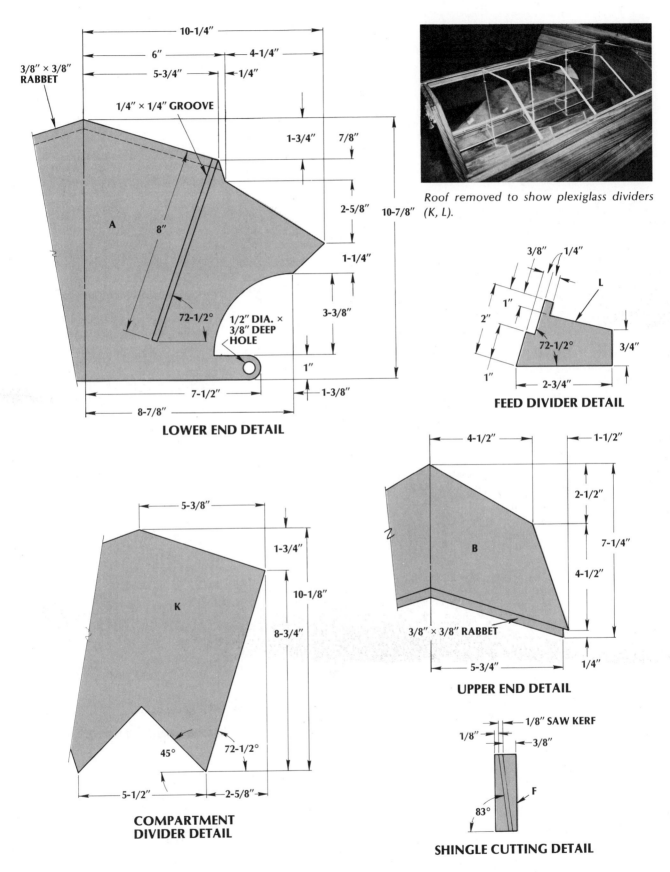

10-1/4"

6" 4-1/4"

3/8" × 3/8"
RABBET

5-3/4" 1/4"

1/4" × 1/4" GROOVE

1-3/4" 7/8"

A 8"

2-5/8" 10-7/8"

72-1/2°

1-1/4"

1/2" DIA. ×
3/8" DEEP
HOLE

3-3/8"

1"

7-1/2" 1-3/8"

8-7/8"

LOWER END DETAIL

Roof removed to show plexiglass dividers (K, L).

3/8" 1/4"

1" L

2"

72-1/2°

1" 3/4"

1" 2-3/4"

FEED DIVIDER DETAIL

4-1/2" 1-1/2"

2-1/2"

B 7-1/4"

4-1/2"

3/8" × 3/8" RABBET

5-3/4" 1/4"

UPPER END DETAIL

5-3/8"

1-3/4"

K 10-1/8"

8-3/4"

45° 72-1/2°

5-1/2" 2-5/8"

**COMPARTMENT
DIVIDER DETAIL**

1/8" SAW KERF

1/8" 3/8"

F

83°

SHINGLE CUTTING DETAIL

17

BANDSAW SCULPTURE

From *HANDS ON* Sept/Oct 79

If you make two sets of cuts that are totally different from each other, you can end up with some fantastic sculptures—animals, people, abstract shapes.

To sculpt with your bandsaw, you have to develop two patterns. Say you want to cut out an animal: Imagine what that animal looks like from the front and draw the outline. Next, imagine what it looks like from the side (or in some cases, the top) and draw that outline. Take care to make each of your drawings exactly the same scale. Use these two outlines as patterns for making a series of compound bandsaw cuts. Once again, make your first piece out of scrap stock to see if your patterns give you what you want.

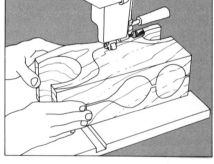

Use a bandsaw to sculpt figures from stock with the outline of the figure drawn on it.

ONE SQUARE = 1"

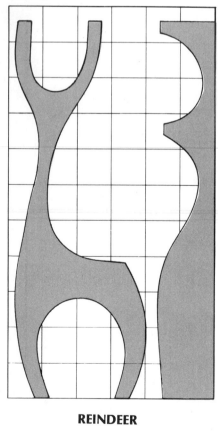

REINDEER

ONE SQUARE = 1"

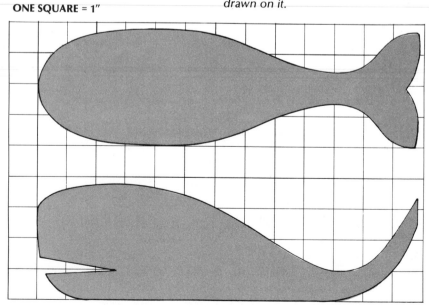

WHALE

There are some projects that you make to give as gifts that you wish you had yourself. This memo pad will be one of those projects. Follow the seven simple steps given below, but be prepared to make at least two!

1. Prepare stock by ripping and jointing a 10" long piece of wood to a 4-1/2" width. Cut a 1/16" deep × 3-1/2" wide × 3-1/2" long stop groove in one end of the piece. Use the dado attachment and a push block for this operation. Resaw the stock to 3/8" thick on the bandsaw.

2. Cut all pieces to size. The 1/16" grooves are in front (B) and back (D) only.

3. Bevel the edges of the writing surface (C) on the disc sander with the table at 45°.

4. Assemble with glue the base (A), front (B), writing surface (C), and back (D).

5. Drill holes for the supports (E).

6. Drill holes in the supports (E) for brads, using a V-block to secure the stock. Next, drill the rod (F) using the horizontal boring mode and the miter gauge for support.

7. Assemble the paper holder by putting brads into the rod (F) and clipping them to length. Press fit the assembly into the base (using no glue), then thread the paper through the slots.

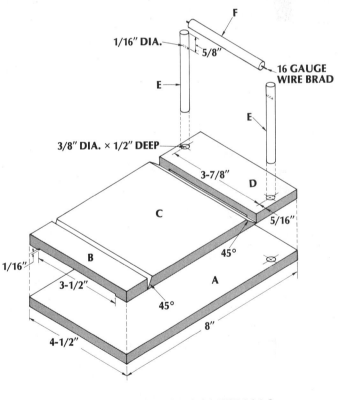

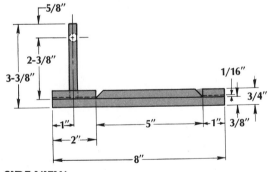

SIDE VIEW

TOP VIEW

LIST OF MATERIALS

(finished dimensions in inches)

A	Base	3/8 × 4-1/2 × 8
B	Front	3/8 × 4-1/2 × 1
C	Writing surface	3/8 × 4-1/2 × 5
D	Back	3/8 × 4-1/2 × 2
E	Supports (2)	3/8 dia. × 3
F	Rod	3/8 dia. × 3-1/2

JEWELRY BOX ▣

From *HANDS ON* July/Aug 82

This simple project is one you'll want to make twice—one to keep and one to give as a sentimental gift. Making a fixture for the over-arm pin router and producing this jewelry box is a snap. Here's how.

1. Cut the stock for the fixture parts (A, B, C, D, E, F) to size according to the List of Materials.
2. Layout the plywood template (A) according to the drawing. Drill the corner curves and cut out the inside waste stock with the jigsaw. File and sand all edges smooth.

3. Drill the holes in one fixture side (C) to accept the T-nuts. Insert the T-nuts into the holes and tap them lightly to seat them in place.
4. Fasten the plywood template (A) to the fixture bottom (B) using #8 × 1″ flathead wood screws. Attach the fixture sides (C) and fixture ends (D) to the fixture bottom using #8 × 1-1/4″ flathead wood screws.
5. Resaw the box lid (G) from the box body (F) using the bandsaw. Set the rip fence to allow a 1/4″ cut. Sand the saw marks from the box body and lid with the belt sander.
6. Clamp the jewelry box body (F) into the fixture assembly, using thumbscrews and the clamp bar (E). Make sure the box body is seated flat and secure in the fixture asembly.
7. Pin rout the box body. Use the router arm with a 3/8″ bit and a 3/8″ guide pin. For safer and easier handling, rout the recesses in three passes.
8. Round the edges by replacing the straight bit with a 1/4″ round over bit. Adjust the depth of the bit to round off all the inside edges of the cavities.
9. Sand and finish the box. Mount the hardware and line the box with felt.

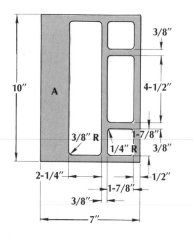

TEMPLATE LAYOUT

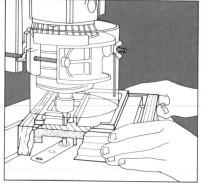

Cutaway view of the pin routing technique.

LIST OF MATERIALS

(finished dimensions in inches)

A	Plywood template	3/8 × 7 × 10
B	Fixture bottom	3/4 × 7 × 10
C	Fixture sides (2)	3/4 × 1-5/8 × 11-1/2
D	Fixture ends (2)	3/4 × 1-5/8 × 7
E	Clamp bar	3/4 × 1 × 10
F	Box body	1-1/4 × 5-1/2 × 10
G	Box lid	1/4 × 5-1/2 × 10

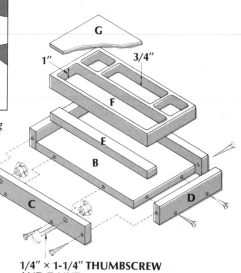

1/4″ × 1-1/4″ THUMBSCREW AND T-NUT

BOX AND FIXTURE ASSEMBLY

PLYWOOD PARQUET

From *HANDS ON* Sept/Oct 81

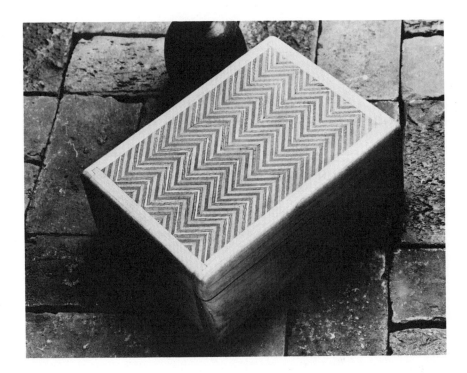

Parquet—inlaying of hardwoods in a pattern—is intricate, time-consuming, and expensive. But you can mimic the look of parquet with plywood.

Simply glue up small blocks of plywood, cut edgewise, in a geometric arrangement.

Any grade or thickness of plywood will work, although construction grade contains many voids. When voids do occur, hide them by first brushing on a varnish and sanding lightly with wet/dry sandpaper. The sawdust from sanding mixes with the varnish to form a paste that fills the cracks. For larger voids, use a wood filler or patching stick.

First construct the box; then, glue plywood parquet (E) to backing (D) of box lid. Belt sand smooth. Cut the lid from the body using a table saw, then mount hinges.

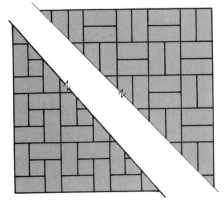

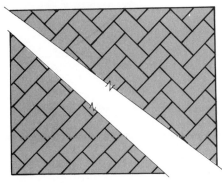

POSSIBLE PARQUET PATTERNS

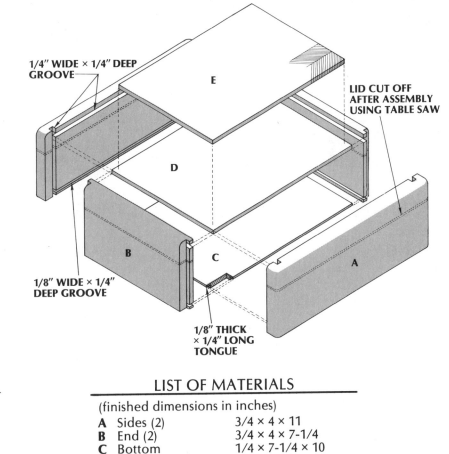

1/4" WIDE × 1/4" DEEP GROOVE

E

LID CUT OFF AFTER ASSEMBLY USING TABLE SAW

D

1/8" WIDE × 1/4" DEEP GROOVE

B

C

A

1/8" THICK × 1/4" LONG TONGUE

LIST OF MATERIALS

(finished dimensions in inches)

A	Sides (2)	3/4 × 4 × 11
B	End (2)	3/4 × 4 × 7-1/4
C	Bottom	1/4 × 7-1/4 × 10
D	Parquet backing	1/4 × 7-1/4 × 10
E	Plywood parquet	1/4 × 6-3/4 × 9-1/2

GAME TABLE

From *HANDS ON* Nov/Dec 82

Y ou can build this beautiful game table following the eight simple steps outlined here. We built this project out of mahogany and used maple and walnut for the checkerboard top.

1. Prepare stock for the legs (A), apron (B), and cleat strips (C) on the table saw. Make sure the stock for the legs is square and straight.

2. Drill dowel holes in the legs (A) and apron (B). Use the drill press for the legs and the horizontal boring mode for the apron pieces. After drilling the holes, be sure to mark all pieces for position.

3. Turn the legs (A) on the lathe following the drawings, or create your own style. Sand the legs while they are still on the lathe.

4. Assemble the legs (A) and apron (B) with dowels and woodworker's glue.

5. Make the checkerboard top by first setting the saw to cut 2″ strips of 3/4″ thick light (F) and dark (G) woods. Glue and clamp these strips together and allow to dry. Square one end and cut 2″ strips across the light and dark wood. Glue and clamp these strips together alternating them to create the checkerboard pattern.

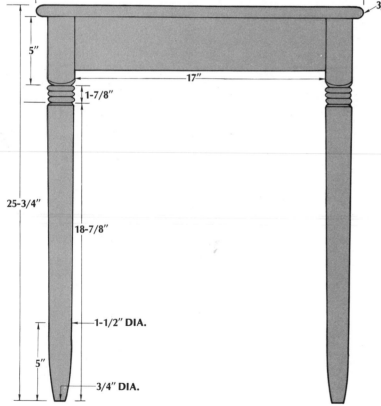

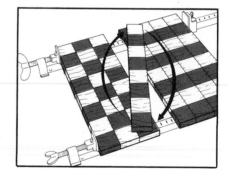

6. Cut the frame pieces (E) for the checkerboard. Cut each piece to approximate length and then use the disc sander to achieve a precision fit. Make the spline grooves and splines for the frame. Glue and clamp one side of the frame at a time to the checkerboard.

7. Attach the cleat strips (C) to the apron with #8 × 1″ flathead wood screws. Cut the bottom (D) out of 1/4″ plywood and secure it to the cleat strip with brads. Mortise the recesses for the hinges.

8. Apply the finish of your choice.

LIST OF MATERIALS

(finished dimensions in inches)

A	Legs (4)	1-3/4 × 1-3/4 × 25
B	Apron pieces (4)	3/4 × 3-1/2 × 17
C	Cleat strips (4)	1/2 × 3/4 × 17
D	Bottom	1/4 × 18-3/4 × 18-3/4
E	Frame pieces (4)	3/4 × 3 × 22
F	Light wood (4)	3/4 × 2 × 18
G	Dark wood (4)	3/4 × 2 × 18

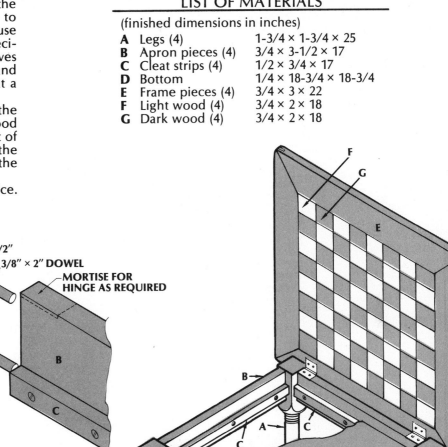

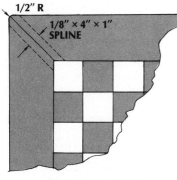

CORNER DETAIL

BANDSAWN CHESS AND CHECKERS

From *HANDS ON* May/June 80

It's an exciting game to play, and an elegant game to watch. Chess is played with six different pieces—king, queen, bishop, knight, rook, and pawn—each piece a tiny sculpture. Most chess sets are turned on a lathe or carved by hand; however, the set pictured here is made on a bandsaw, each piece formed with a compound cut.

MAKING COMPOUND CUTS

Here's the technique of making compound cuts.
1. Make your first cut or cuts.
2. Tape the cut pieces back together.
3. Turn the workpiece 90° and cut again.
When you unwrap the tape, you'll have a three-dimensional wooden shape. It's a simple technique, but we suggest that for this project you modify step 2 to make it even simpler.

Instead of taping the pieces back together, leave about 1/8" of stock uncut underneath the head of each chess piece. This will keep the

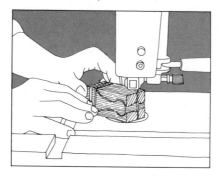 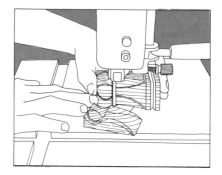

When cutting chess pieces, leave 1/8" of stock uncut underneath the head, then knock off scrap.

scrap attached with no need to tape it back on.

When you've made all your cuts, go back and saw the remaining 1/8" segments, knocking off the scrap. Only when making your last

1/8" cut will you need any of that scrap, and then you still don't have to tape it back on. Just set the chess piece on top to make the cut square with the blade.

This modification of the compound cuts technique works well for most small workpieces and saves a great deal of time.

MAKING THE CHESS PIECES

Select two contrasting woods to distinguish one side of the chess set from the other. We chose to make our set from walnut and maple.

Cut your wood into small blocks before starting on the compound cuts. Check the List of Materials for the number and size of blocks you'll need.

The kings, queens, rooks, and pawns (A, B, E, F) are shaped with two cuts, each exactly the same as the other. So are the bishops (C),

but on the second cut put a kerf in the heads to form the bishop's miter. The knights are made with two different cuts to form the traditional horse heads. You may want to round their noses slightly to make them appear more horse-like.

LIST OF MATERIALS

(finished dimensions in inches)

A	Kings (2)	2 × 2 × 5-1/4
B	Queens (2)	2 × 2 × 4-3/4
C	Bishops (4)	1-3/4 × 1-3/4 × 4-1/8
D	Knights (4)	1-3/4 × 1-3/4 × 3-1/2
E	Rooks (4)	1-3/4 × 1-3/4 × 4
F	Pawns (16)	1-1/2 × 1-1/2 × 3-1/8

CHECKERS

If you want to add checkers to your chess set, cut or glue up two blocks 1-3/4" × 1-3/4" × 12", each block made from one of your contrasting woods. Turn the blocks on a lathe to form two cylinders 1-3/4" in diameter. Cut checkers to size with a bandsaw.

FINISHING THE PIECES

The shapes of the various chess pieces are fairly intricate and tedious to sand. However, a set of small drum sanders speeds up sanding considerably. The drums reach into most of the curves and crevices, and the chess pieces require only touch-up hand-sanding. If you decide to sand the chess set by hand, a small half-round rasp and a supply of emery boards will prove useful.

Dip the chess pieces and checkers in a can of high-gloss polyurethane wood finish. Wipe off the excess with a rag, and let dry on a sheet of wax paper. Dip the pieces again and wait for the finish to get tacky (about 10 to 15 minutes). Rub the partially dried finish into the wood with a rag. Don't worry if this rag becomes gummed up; this actually helps buff the finish. Let the pieces stand overnight to harden completely.

Rubbing the gummy polyurethane into the wood fills any mill marks and surface imperfections. The wood becomes glass smooth and takes on a soft glow. After the second coat, the polyurethane looks remarkably like a hand-rubbed oil finish, with only a fraction of the hand-rubbing.

Finally, glue felt to the underside of the chess pieces and checkers to protect the board they will rest on. And that's it, except for finding yourself a chess partner to help break the set in.

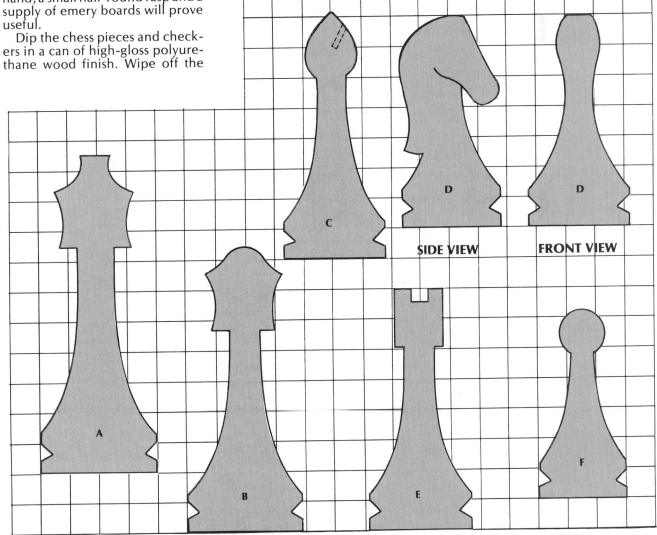

SIDE VIEW   FRONT VIEW

TURNED CHESS SET

From *HANDS ON* Jan/Feb 82

When you're finished with this project, you'll have a game to enjoy and a keepsake to treasure for many years. This chess set is a challenging project that can be made from a very small amount of wood.

1. Prepare about 9' of 1-3/8" stock. Cut the turning stock to size according to the List of Materials. Leave an extra 1" on all the lengths for waste stock. Select contrasting light and dark hardwoods such as maple or birch and mahogany or walnut. Mark the centers on all ends.

2. Turn all the pieces except the knights (C) according to the patterns shown. For best results, use a set of miniature woodturning chisels.

3. Turn the knights (C), forming the base and part of the head. Set the stock 3/8" off-center. Turn the neck of the knight and sand the neck smooth. Move the knight back on-center and finish turning the head, stopping just before cutting the piece free.

4. Cut the bishop's kerf with a bandsaw. The king's cross is also cut on the bandsaw. To make the rook's crown, first drill a 3/4" diameter × 1/8" deep hole in the top of the rook. Then, using the bandsaw, cut the 1/8" deep × 1/8" wide crown slots.

5. Apply the finish of your choice to the chess pieces. Finally, glue felt onto the bottoms of all pieces.

LIST OF MATERIALS

(finished dimensions in inches)

A	Kings (2)	1-3/8 dia. × 4-3/8
B	Queens (2)	1-3/8 dia. × 4-1/8
C	Knights (4)	1-3/8 dia. × 3-1/8
D	Bishops (4)	1-3/8 dia. × 3-3/8
E	Rooks (4)	1-3/8 dia. × 2-3/8
F	Pawns (16)	1-3/8 dia. × 2-1/8

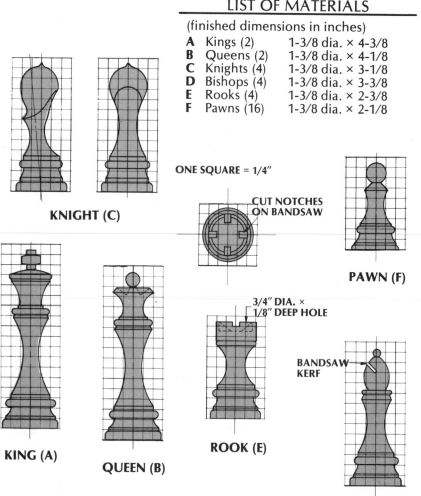

KNIGHT (C)

ONE SQUARE = 1/4"

CUT NOTCHES ON BANDSAW

PAWN (F)

3/4" DIA. × 1/8" DEEP HOLE

BANDSAW KERF

KING (A)

QUEEN (B)

ROOK (E)

BISHOP (D)

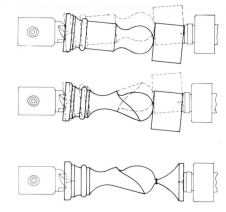

Turning a knight.

From *HANDS ON* July/Aug 80

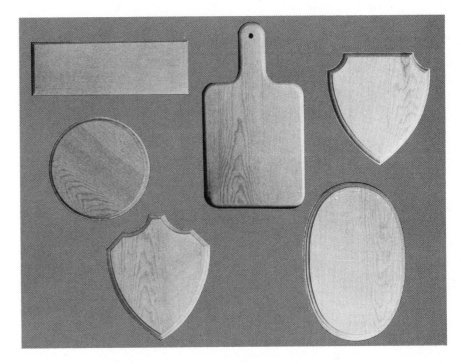

Plaques and picture frames always make a great gift and they can be made quickly and inexpensively. You can even mount pictures, decals, slogans, etc. on them. Make plaques individually by using the bandsaw or jigsaw to cut out shapes. Edges are formed using the shaper. If you want to mass produce plaques, follow the steps below.

1. Make templates of the designs you want. Trace that template and make a fixture. (Some square or rectangular plaques can be cut without fixtures.)

2. Cut blanks and attach to fixtures, using two nails or screws.

3. Cut out the shape on a bandsaw or jigsaw; then, remove the plaque or picture frame from the fixture.

4. Shape the edges, using the router or shaper. If you're making a picture frame, remember to cut a rabbet in the back.

5. Sand the face and edges of the plaques and frames with a belt sander.

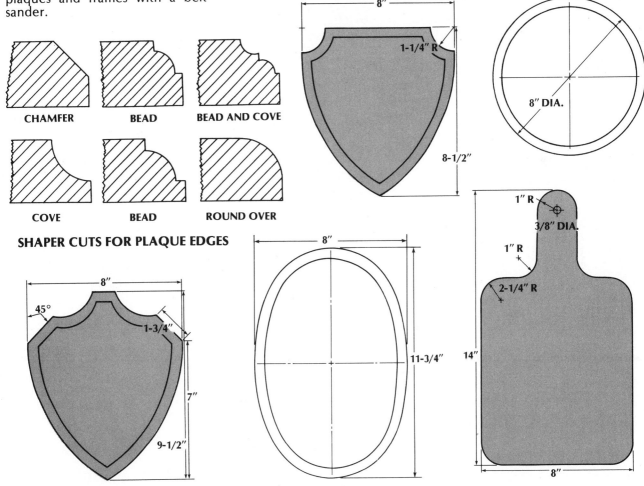

CHAMFER   BEAD   BEAD AND COVE

COVE   BEAD   ROUND OVER

SHAPER CUTS FOR PLAQUE EDGES

WHALE BOX

From *HANDS ON* July/Aug 80

Trace these whale patterns on 3-1/2″ × 3-1/2″ × 12″ blocks. Cut the top contour first on your bandsaw. Tape the pieces back together and turn the wood 90°. Cut the side contour, doing the drawer last.

Mount the drawer in the drilling fixture and drill out the compartment with a large multi-spur bit. Round the edges of the drawer and the whale with a file or flutter sheets. Sand all surfaces with a drum sander. Apply finish and glue felt in the bottom of the drawer compartment.

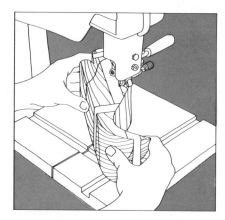

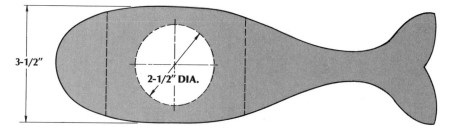

TOP VIEW

3-1/2″

2-1/2″ DIA.

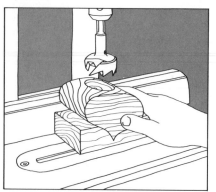

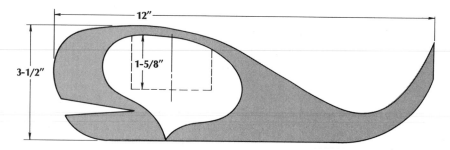

SIDE VIEW

12″

3-1/2″

1-5/8″

CANDLE SCONCE

From *HANDS ON* Nov/Dec 83

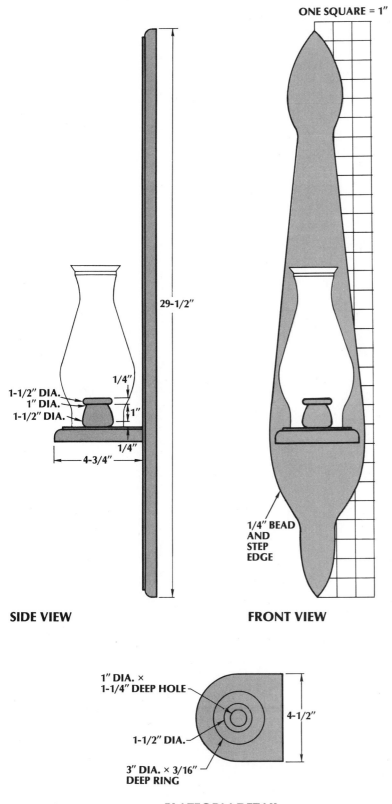

ONE SQUARE = 1"

29-1/2"

1-1/2" DIA.
1" DIA.
1-1/2" DIA.

1/4"

1"

1/4"

4-3/4"

SIDE VIEW

1/4" BEAD
AND
STEP
EDGE

FRONT VIEW

1" DIA. ×
1-1/4" DEEP HOLE

1-1/2" DIA.

3" DIA. × 3/16"
DEEP RING

4-1/2"

PLATFORM DETAIL

Make one of these beautiful sconces to hang by a door or make two pairs to grace both sides of a hall mirror.

Transfer the pattern onto 3/4" stock and cut out the basic shape for the back with the bandsaw or jigsaw. Mount the 3/4" × 4-1/2" × 5" piece of stock for the platform on the screw center and turn the 3/16" deep ring for the chimney glass (available at most department stores) in the center with the parting tool. Cut the platform to shape with the bandsaw. Next, mount a 2" length of 1-1/2" square stock to the screw center and turn the candle cup. Use the disc sander to smooth the outside contours of the sconce pieces. Shape the edges of the pieces with a 1/4" round over bit on the shaper or router. Attach the platform to the back with #10 × 1-1/2" flathead wood screws, then glue and attach the candle cup with a #8 × 1-1/4" flathead wood screw and glue.

BIRD MOBILE

From *HANDS ON* July/Aug 80

Mobiles add poetic motion to most any room. Start by making a masonite template of the bird design and trace on 3-1/2" thick blocks.

Before cutting out the design, drill a 1/8" hole where indicated on the pattern. Then, cut out the outside contour on your bandsaw and sand off the millmarks with a strip sander. Resaw the stock into 1/4" thick pieces and sand the surfaces.

Finish with oil, stain, or paint. Cut fishing line to length, and tie the lines to the birds and the crossbars (1/8" or 3/16" dowel rods). Move the lines back and forth on the crossbars until the birds are balanced.

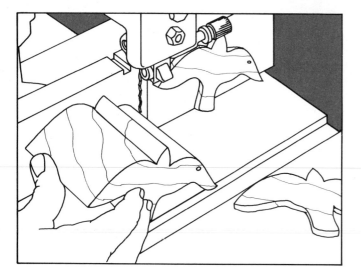

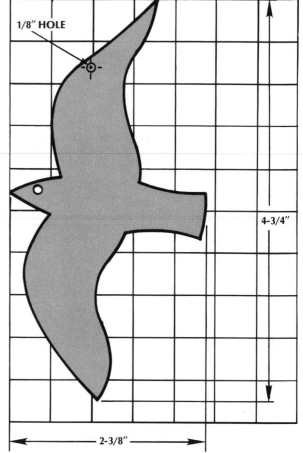

ONE SQUARE = 1/2"

1/8" HOLE

4-3/4"

2-3/8"

From *HANDS ON* Jan/Feb 81

This candleholder can be used as a decorative accent. It conveniently holds a standard size warmer candle cup and is small enough to even slip under a fondue pot.

Just cut a 2 × 4 into blocks that are 4-1/8″ long. Glue two blocks together face-to-face to form a 3″ × 3-1/2″ × 4-1/8″ block.

Using the table saw and miter gauge set at 60°, cut the corners off the block to form the hexagon shape.

Then with the drill press and two large size drills (multi-spur bit or Forstner bit), drill 1-1/4″ diameter holes in the center of each of the six sides and the large hole 2-1/2″ diameter nearly through the top to fit the warmer cup.

Sand all flat surfaces with the disc sander. Stain and finish.

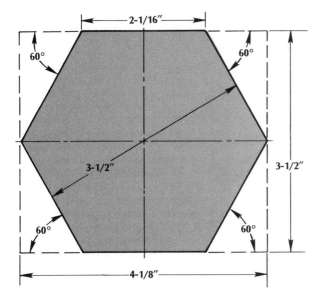

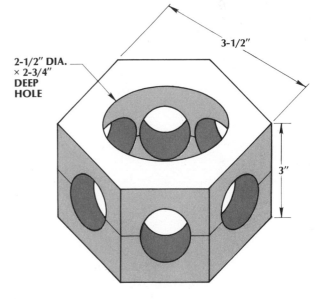

Kitchen
Projects

Projects for the kitchen have always provided a source of enjoyment for the home woodworker. The beauty of wood enhances any kitchen, and the use of wooden cooking utensils adds elegance to any entertaining. Here are over twenty projects that will be sure to provide the woodworker with hours of enjoyment...and the cook with hours of use.

SPAGHETTI MEASURE

From *HANDS ON* Apr/May/June 83

1-3/4" DIA.

1-1/2" DIA.

1-1/8" DIA.

7/8" DIA.

3/8" DIA.

Getting the right amount of spaghetti is easy with this simple-to-make kitchen utensil. You can measure the correct amount of spaghetti every time for one to four servings.

Resaw 3" wide × 15" long hardwood stock to 3/8" thick and lay out the pattern and hole positions. Drill the holes before you cut out the contour. Use 3/8" and 7/8" brad point bits and 1-1/8", 1-1/2", and 1-3/4" hole saws. Cut out the pattern on a jigsaw or bandsaw. Round off all the edges and the rims of the holes on both sides. Sand, then apply a nontoxic finish or leave unfinished.

To make this on a router arm, use 3/8" plywood to make the pattern. Attach the pattern to 3/8" stock and rout out the shape and holes with a 3/8" straight bit. A 3/16" round over bit shapes the edges.

ONE SQUARE = 1/2"

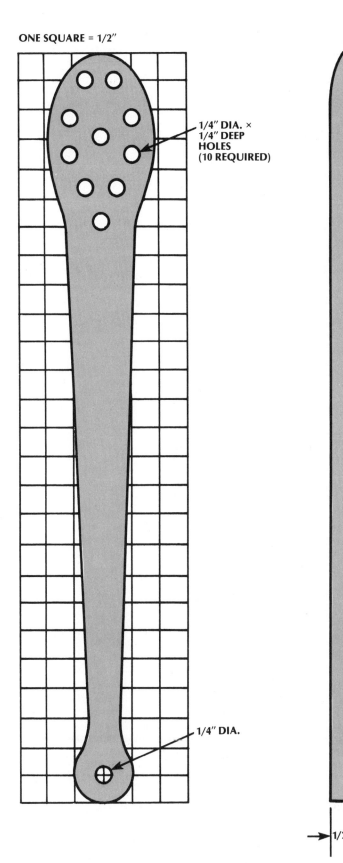

1/4" DIA. ×
1/4" DEEP
HOLES
(10 REQUIRED)

1/4" DIA. ×
1-1/4" LONG
PEGS
(10 REQUIRED)

1/4" DIA.

1/2"

This project will solve the cook's problem of how to conveniently serve pasta at dinner time. Take a 1/2" × 2" × 13" piece of hardwood stock and lay out the pattern and peg positions. Drill the peg holes 1/4" deep. Cut out the contour on the bandsaw or jigsaw. Glue in the pegs with a waterproof glue. Round the back of the fork on the disc and drum sanders. Apply a nontoxic finish or leave natural.

COOLING RACKS

From *HANDS ON* Apr/May/June 83

Few things smell as good as fresh baked bread. Bakeries, however, have made it so easy to get fresh bread that homemade bread usually appears only on a holiday. To encourage more baking at home, here are some simple and beautiful cooling racks that you can make in the time it takes to bake a loaf or two.

Cut the sides to length using hardwood from your scrap pile. Drill the 3/8" diameter × 1/4" deep holes in the sides for the dowel rods. Sand the sides and round all the edges with the belt sander or a hand sander. Next, lightly sand dowel rods, then cut them to length. Use the bandsaw or a miter box. Chamfer the ends of the rods with the disc sander. Assemble the rack with glue and clamp it with bar clamps. Apply a nontoxic finish or leave natural.

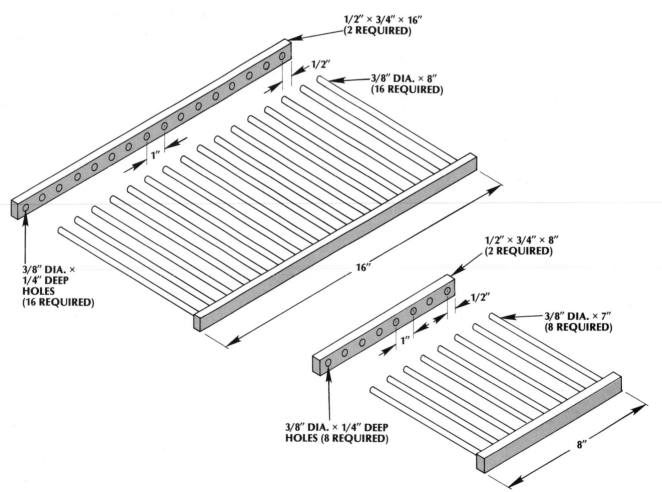

1/2" × 3/4" × 16"
(2 REQUIRED)

1/2"

3/8" DIA. × 8"
(16 REQUIRED)

1"

3/8" DIA. ×
1/4" DEEP
HOLES
(16 REQUIRED)

16"

1/2" × 3/4" × 8"
(2 REQUIRED)

1/2"

3/8" DIA. × 7"
(8 REQUIRED)

1"

3/8" DIA. × 1/4" DEEP
HOLES (8 REQUIRED)

8"

Few kitchen utensils are more popular than this kitchen doofer. This ingenious device hooks on to an oven rack to push it in or pull it out, saving burned fingers and singed pot holders. Make one with a bandsaw or jigsaw or make many with a router arm. Here's how to set up for the router arm.

To make the template, first trace the doofer pattern on 3/8" stock. Using a 3/8" drill, drill holes for the push/pull notches. With the bandsaw, cut out template to the shape of the doofer and sand with a drum sander.

From a sink cutout, cut out the fixture and attach the template to the particleboard side using 1" brads. Then with a 3/8" router bit and 3/8" pin, rout the groove in the plastic laminated side. This groove is best made in three 1/8" cuts, each cut 1/8" deeper than the preceding.

Cut doofer stock and attach to fixture. Alignment marks on the fixture are useful here. Rout out the doofer making two or more cuts if your stock is thicker than 1/4". Drill the handle hole and sand with disc and drum sanders.

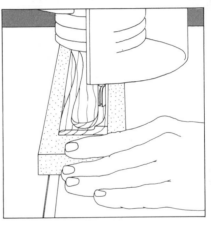

Make the doofer on a router arm.

ONE SQUARE = 1/2"

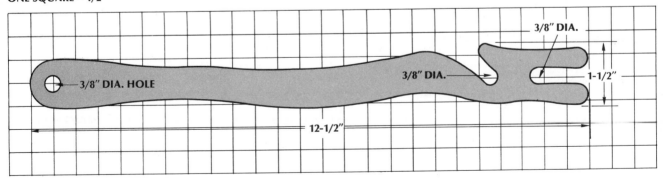

3/8" DIA.

3/8" DIA. HOLE

3/8" DIA.

1-1/2"

12-1/2"

MEAT PLATTER RA

From *HANDS ON* Apr/May 81

This decorative meat platter looks good sitting on the table or hung on the wall. Small gutters, arranged in the shape of a tree, channel the drippings into a trough at one end of the platter and keep them from spilling over onto the tablecloth.

With a jigsaw, cut a pattern from a piece of hardboard and attach it to the unlaminated side of a sink cutout. With a 3/8" straight bit in your overarm router, pin rout a template in the cutout. On the trough end of this template, attach a 1/4" thick strip of wood. When you rout the platters, this strip will tilt the stock so that the gutters will all run downhill into the trough.

Glue up 3/4" stock for the platters using a waterproof glue. If you want, alternate dark and light colored bands of wood. When the glue sets, sand the surface smooth and attach the stock to the template. Pin rout the inside (tree-shaped) gutters with a 3/8" core box bit, and the outside gutter and trough with a 3/4" core box bit. Finally, cut the outside shape with a 3/8" straight bit.

Finish with salad bowl finish or mineral oil.

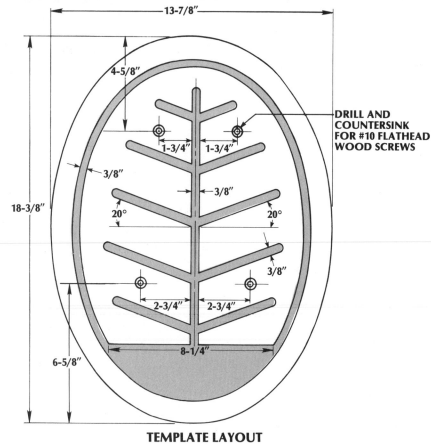

TEMPLATE LAYOUT

DRILL AND COUNTERSINK FOR #10 FLATHEAD WOOD SCREWS

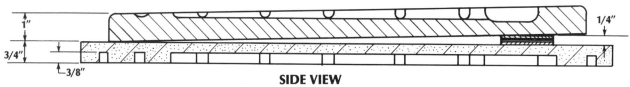

SIDE VIEW

Here is a set of salt and pepper shakers that you'll really enjoy making and using. Turn one at a time or several sets at a time out of a full 2 × 2 or glued-up stock (allow glued-up stock to remain clamped for at least 24 hours). Turn the shakers so the bases are toward the quill. If you turn more than one at a time, you'll need to leave approximately 1/2" of stock between each shaker. After you have turned the outside contour, turn off the machine and remove the tool rest and turning. Mount the saw table, then remount the turning. Raise the table level with the bottom of the stock. Set the miter gauge next to the stock and tighten the miter gauge locking screw. Release the stock from the lathe by retracting the quill, and mount the drill chuck. Using Forstner bits, counterbore and drill the inside of the shakers. If you turned more than one at a time, cut off the end shaker and repeat the boring operation for the next shaker. Sand the ends of the shakers smooth and drill the 3/32" shaker holes. Apply finish to the outside surface only. Insert cork stoppers (available at hardware stores).

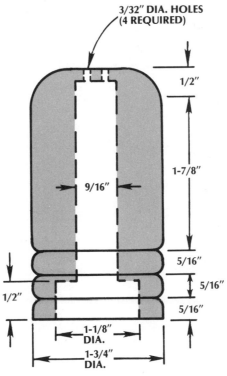

3/32" DIA. HOLES
(4 REQUIRED)

1/2"

1-7/8"

9/16"

5/16"

5/16"

5/16"

1/2"

1-1/8"
DIA.

1-3/4"
DIA.

ROOSTER TRIVET

From *HANDS ON* Nov/Dec 83

This uniquely designed trivet makes a good gift for cooks who enjoy serving casseroles hot from the oven or just need a place to set a hot skillet.

To make this trivet, prepare a 1/2″ × 7-1/2″ × 8-1/4″ blank of hardwood—cherry, walnut, etc. Transfer the pattern to the blank. Drill holes in each of the sections to be cut out. Only one hole is necessary but a series of holes will reduce cutting time. Use a backup board to prevent chip-out on the backside. Cut the outside and inside contours on the jigsaw and file the edges smooth with pattern files. Apply a penetrating oil finish or leave plain.

ONE SQUARE = 1/2″

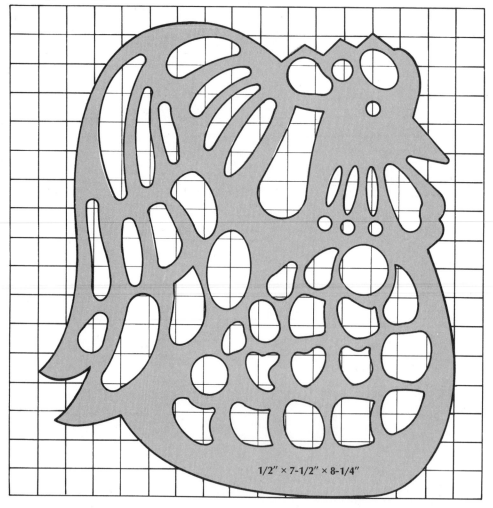

1/2″ × 7-1/2″ × 8-1/4″

This project will prevent countless finger burns when moving the oven rack in or out. The "kitchen fish" has a "mouth" that pushes hot oven racks in and a "gill cover" that pulls them out. And, when the fish is not in use, it makes an attractive decoration on the kitchen wall.

To make four of these fish at one time, tape together two pieces of 3/4" × 5" × 14-1/2" stock. Transfer the design from the drawing to the stock and then drill the 3/16" diameter tail hole. Next, cut out the design on the bandsaw. Resaw the stock to 3/8" and sand the surface smooth.

Make the eyes by using a round-tipped punch and hammer, or drill a small countersink with a 3/16" twist bit.

The scales are formed with a 1" wood chisel and a mallet. (It's a good idea to first practice this on scrap stock.)

Sand the project with the drum sander and round the edges by hand with fine sandpaper. Highlight the eyes and scales with stain; then, apply the finish of your choice.

ONE SQUARE = 1/2"

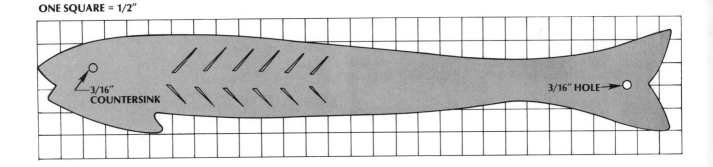

3/16"
COUNTERSINK

3/16" HOLE

HERB CLOCK

From *HANDS ON* May/June 81

Here's an interesting kitchen clock filled with good things from the earth—seeds, grains, and herbs. This is a great project because of the variety, no two have to be alike. You can buy dried herbs at a natural foods store, and the clockworks are available at craft/hobby stores or by mail order.

Select a fine hardwood for the face of the clock. The body can be made from inexpensive pine. To make this on the router arm, make two pin routing fixtures; the first (Fixture 1) to cut the clock face (C) and cavities, and the second (Fixture 2) to make the rabbets for the glazing (B) and the clock face, and to cut the hole for the clock motor.

To make the face (C), attach 1/2" thick hardwood to Fixture 1. With a 3/8" pin and straight bit, rout the shapes shown. Switch to a 3/8" piloted round over bit (and no pin), and round all the edges of the clock face. Lay it aside and attach Fixture 1 to the body stock. Again working with the 3/8" pin and straight bit, cut the cavities approximately 1" deep. Remount the body on Fixture 2 and cut the rabbets and the hole.

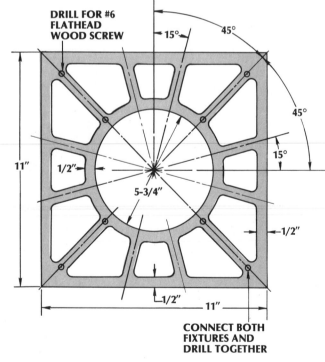

DRILL FOR #6 FLATHEAD WOOD SCREW

15° 45° 45° 15°

11" 11"

1/2" 5-3/4" 1/2"

1/2" 11"

CONNECT BOTH FIXTURES AND DRILL TOGETHER

FIXTURE 1

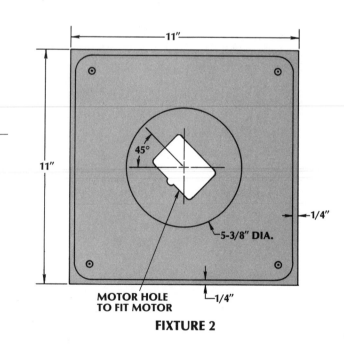

11"

45°

11"

1/4"

5-3/8" DIA.

1/4"

MOTOR HOLE TO FIT MOTOR

FIXTURE 2

Cut the glazing (B) (we used clear acrylic plastic) and drill five holes, one in the center for the clock post and four in the corners where the face (C) will attach to the body (A). Put the clock motor in place, fill the cavities with herbs, and assemble the pieces. Use #6 brass flathead wood screws to attach the face to the body.

LIST OF MATERIALS

(finished dimensions in inches)

A	Body	1-1/2 × 11 × 11
B	Glazing	1/8 × 10-1/2 × 10-1/2
C	Face	1/2 × 11 × 11

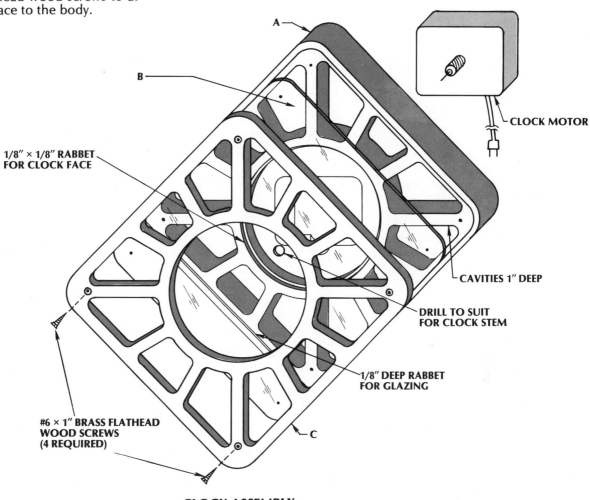

A

B

CLOCK MOTOR

1/8″ × 1/8″ RABBET
FOR CLOCK FACE

CAVITIES 1″ DEEP

DRILL TO SUIT
FOR CLOCK STEM

1/8″ DEEP RABBET
FOR GLAZING

#6 × 1″ BRASS FLATHEAD
WOOD SCREWS
(4 REQUIRED)

C

CLOCK ASSEMBLY

SALT BOX

From *HANDS ON* Nov/Dec 80

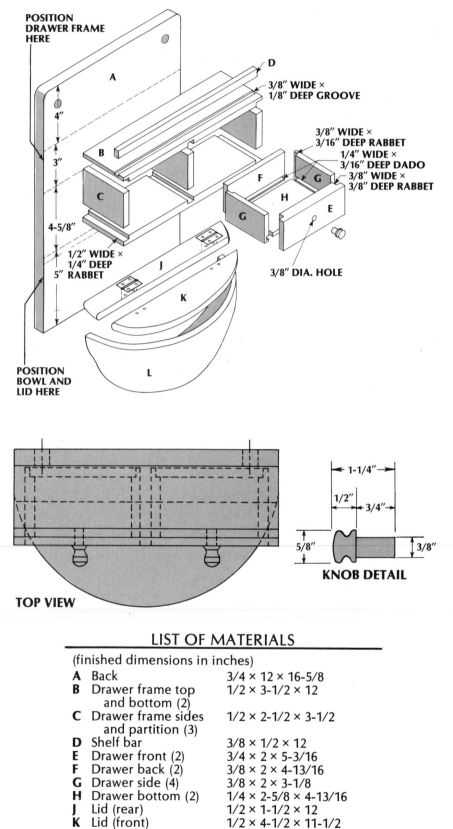

POSITION DRAWER FRAME HERE

A

D

3/8" WIDE × 1/8" DEEP GROOVE

3/8" WIDE × 3/16" DEEP RABBET
1/4" WIDE × 3/16" DEEP DADO
3/8" WIDE × 3/8" DEEP RABBET

B

4"

3"

C

F

G

H

G

E

4-5/8"

1/2" WIDE × 1/4" DEEP RABBET
5"

J

K

3/8" DIA. HOLE

POSITION BOWL AND LID HERE

L

TOP VIEW

1-1/4"
1/2"
3/4"
5/8"
3/8"

KNOB DETAIL

Not so many years ago, cooks kept a box of coarse salt near the cookstove to season soups, stews, or whatever was cooking. These antiques are still handy, but now they're used to hold matches, coupons, and many small items you have nowhere to keep.

Start this project by cutting and gluing up rings for a large bowl 11" in diameter. Allow bowl to remain clamped for 24 hours before turning. Glue up 3/4" thick stock for the back.

Resaw stock to thicknesses you need for the other parts—1/2", 3/8", and 1/4". Cut all pieces to size.

Using a dado blade or router accessory, cut joinery in drawer pieces and drawer frame. Glue up drawers and drawer frame.

Turn the wooden bowl and drawer knobs. Using a piece of masking tape, mark a straight line down the middle of the bowl. Saw the bowl in half on the bandsaw.

Glue the bowl and the drawer frame to the back and reinforce with #10 × 1-1/4" flathead wood screws. Hinge the lid pieces together and glue the rear piece to the lip of the bowl. Drill the drawer front for knobs, glue knobs in holes, and slide drawers in place. If you want, round the edges of the lid, drawers, and drawer frame with a rasp. Finish the project with oil or salad bowl finish.

What do you do with the other half of the bowl? Another Salt Box—they make unique gifts.

LIST OF MATERIALS

(finished dimensions in inches)

A	Back	3/4 × 12 × 16-5/8
B	Drawer frame top and bottom (2)	1/2 × 3-1/2 × 12
C	Drawer frame sides and partition (3)	1/2 × 2-1/2 × 3-1/2
D	Shelf bar	3/8 × 1/2 × 12
E	Drawer front (2)	3/4 × 2 × 5-3/16
F	Drawer back (2)	3/8 × 2 × 4-13/16
G	Drawer side (4)	3/8 × 2 × 3-1/8
H	Drawer bottom (2)	1/4 × 2-5/8 × 4-13/16
J	Lid (rear)	1/2 × 1-1/2 × 12
K	Lid (front)	1/2 × 4-1/2 × 11-1/2
L	Bowl (1/2)	11 dia. × 4-1/2

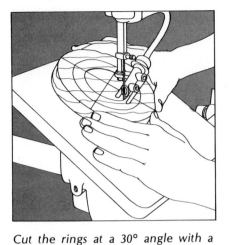

Cut the rings at a 30° angle with a jigsaw.

Turn the bowl.

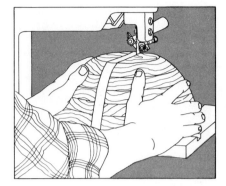

Make a straight line with masking tape to aid in cutting bowl in two.

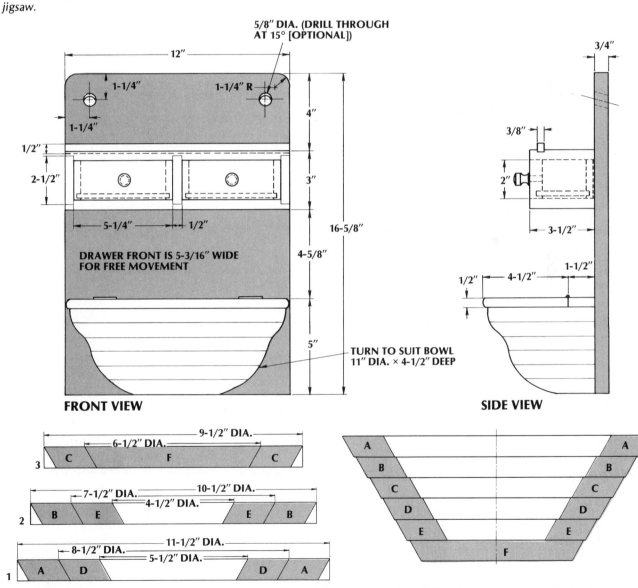

5/8" DIA. (DRILL THROUGH AT 15° [OPTIONAL])

12"

1-1/4"

1-1/4"

1-1/4" R

4"

1/2"

2-1/2"

3"

5-1/4"

1/2"

16-5/8"

DRAWER FRONT IS 5-3/16" WIDE FOR FREE MOVEMENT

4-5/8"

5"

TURN TO SUIT BOWL 11" DIA. × 4-1/2" DEEP

FRONT VIEW

3/4"

3/8"

2"

3-1/2"

1-1/2"

1/2"

4-1/2"

SIDE VIEW

9-1/2" DIA.

6-1/2" DIA.

3

C   F   C

7-1/2" DIA.

10-1/2" DIA.

4-1/2" DIA.

2

B   E   E   B

8-1/2" DIA.

11-1/2" DIA.

5-1/2" DIA.

1

A   D   D   A

Make these cuts in three pieces of stock. Note: All stock is three-quarter inches thick.

A   A
B   B
C   C
D   D
E   E
F

Detail showing ring assembly for bowl.

KNIFE BLOCK CUTTING BOARD

From *HANDS ON* Nov/Dec 80

Here's a simple project that combines two very useful kitchen accessories, a knife block and a cutting board. Not only is this project very handy, but it's also a beautiful kitchen wall decoration.

1. Prepare the stock. Resaw 3/4" stock to make the back (D) and the bottom (E). Glue up the stock to make the back (D), the knife block (C), and the cutting board (A). Use waterproof resorcinol glue. Scrub off the excess glue after clamping pressure has been applied.

2. Resaw the knife block according to the List of Materials. Using the belt sander, sand all resawed parts smooth.

3. Cut the remaining parts to size according to the List of Materials.

4. Cut the joinery in the sides (B) and the knife block (C) using dado blades. When using the dado blade, you'll have to do some hand work where the 3/4" groove meets the 1/2" dado on the side.

5. Round the corners on the back (D), sides (B), and cutting board (A).

6. Cut knife slots in the knife block using the bandsaw.

7. Assemble parts (B, C, D, E) with resorcinol glue.

8. Rout the juice trough. On one end of the cutting board, rout a 3/4" wide × 3/8" deep trough. On the other three sides, rout a 1/2" wide by 3/8" deep trough. Use a core box router bit and a router guide for this operation.

9. Apply the finish. Use a nontoxic finish such as mineral oil or salad bowl finish.

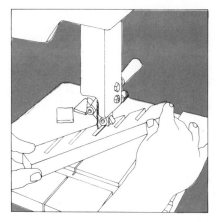

Cut the slots in the knife block with a bandsaw.

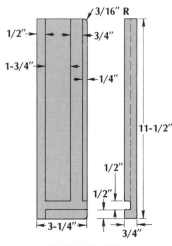

SIDE DETAIL

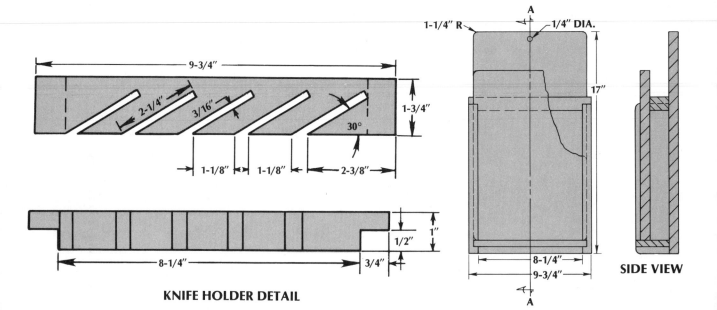

KNIFE HOLDER DETAIL

SIDE VIEW

CUTTING BOARDS

From *HANDS ON* Jan/Feb/Mar 83

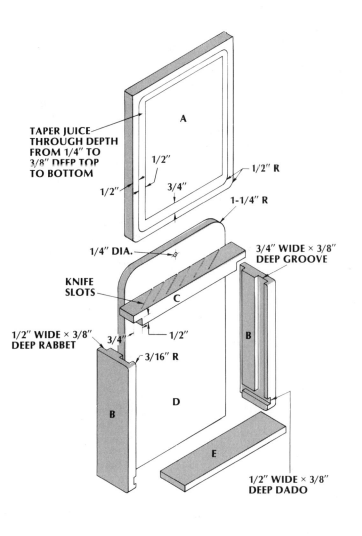

TAPER JUICE THROUGH DEPTH FROM 1/4" TO 3/8" DEEP TOP TO BOTTOM

1/2"

A

1/2"

3/4"

1/2" R

1-1/4" R

1/4" DIA.

3/4" WIDE × 3/8" DEEP GROOVE

KNIFE SLOTS

C

1/2" WIDE × 3/8" DEEP RABBET

3/4"

1/2"

3/16" R

B

B

D

E

1/2" WIDE × 3/8" DEEP DADO

LIST OF MATERIALS

(finished dimensions in inches)

A	Cutting board	3/4 × 9 × 13-1/4
B	Sides (2)	3/4 × 3-1/4 × 11-1/2
C	Knife block	1 × 1-3/4 × 9-3/4
D	Back	1/2 × 9 × 17
E	Bottom	1/2 × 2-1/2 × 9

Cutting boards are always quick and easy. They're even easier with a thickness planer. You need to follow only a few guidelines.

Select close-grained woods such as maple and cherry. Arrange the boards so that the grain of each is going in the same direction. Vertical annual rings, where possible, are best. Use a waterproof glue, such as resorcinol or plastic resin glue. Scrub off all excess glue with a wet shop cloth *before* it dries. Leaving any hard glue on the stock and then running it through the planer will nick and chip the knives.

You can use the router arm with a pin routing fixture to make multiples of the same shape. A core box router bit can be used to form a gutter around the edge. Select any one of a variety of bits for a decorative edge treatment.

After planing and shaping, apply a nontoxic finish such as salad bowl finish or mineral oil.

Clamp up stock for a breadboard. Scrub off all excess glue before it dries.

From *HANDS ON* Jan/Feb 84

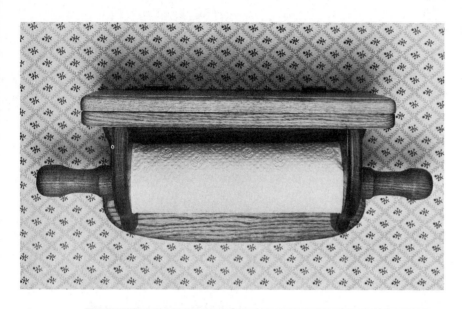

Most small repair jobs in a home don't take place in the shop; they occur on-site. Instead of making a trip to the shop for a hammer or screwdriver every time the need arises, here's an idea for a kitchen toolbox. This handy accessory doubles as a paper towel rack and tool storage area.

1. Cut all parts (A, B, C, D, F) to size according to the List of Materials.

2. Transfer the patterns from the drawings to the stock and cut out contours with the bandsaw. Sand the contours on the drum and disc sanders.

Drill the 1" diameter holes in the sides (A) for the towel bar (F).

3. Make the template for the recessed top (C) and lid (D). Draw the inside contour of the lid on a piece of 3/8" plywood. Drill 3/4" holes in the corners of the contour, then, cut the inside out with the jigsaw. Center the template on the stock and attach it with double-faced carpet tape or brads.

4. Pin rout the top (C) and lid (D) using the overarm router with a 1/2" diameter pin and a 1/2" diameter core box router bit. Make two or three passes to complete the recess.

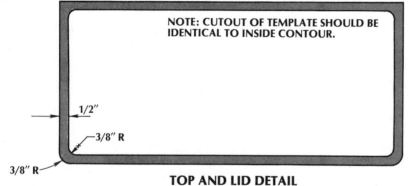

NOTE: CUTOUT OF TEMPLATE SHOULD BE IDENTICAL TO INSIDE CONTOUR.

1/2"

3/8" R

3/8" R

TOP AND LID DETAIL

ONE SQUARE = 1"

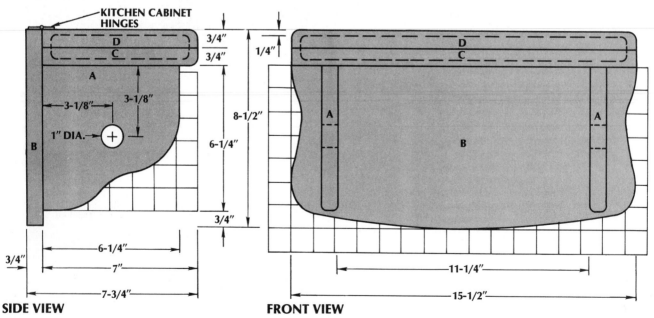

KITCHEN CABINET HINGES

D
C
3/4"
3/4"
1/4"

A

3-1/8"
3-1/8"

1" DIA.

B

8-1/2"

6-1/4"

3/4"

6-1/4"

3/4"

7"

7-3/4"

SIDE VIEW

D
C

A

B

A

11-1/4"

15-1/2"

FRONT VIEW

5. Turn both handles (E) at one time and finish sand them while they are still on the lathe. Cut the handles apart with the bandsaw and drill a 15/16″ diameter × 3/4″ deep hole in the end of each handle. Sand the ends of the towel bar (F) on the disc or belt sander until you achieve a snug fit with the handles.

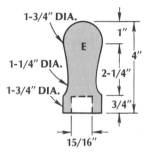

1-3/4″ DIA.

1-1/4″ DIA.

1-3/4″ DIA.

E

1″

4″

2-1/4″

3/4″

15/16″

HANDLE DETAIL

6. Shape the edges of the sides (A), top (C), lid (D), and back (B) with the pin router or with the shaper. Use a quarter round bit on the router or select the profile that you want.

7. Assemble the towel holder by attaching the sides (A) to the back (B) with #9 × 1-1/2″ flathead wood screws. Next, glue the top (C) onto the sides. The lid (D) is attached to the back with kitchen cabinet hinges.

Finish sand the project and apply the finish of your choice.

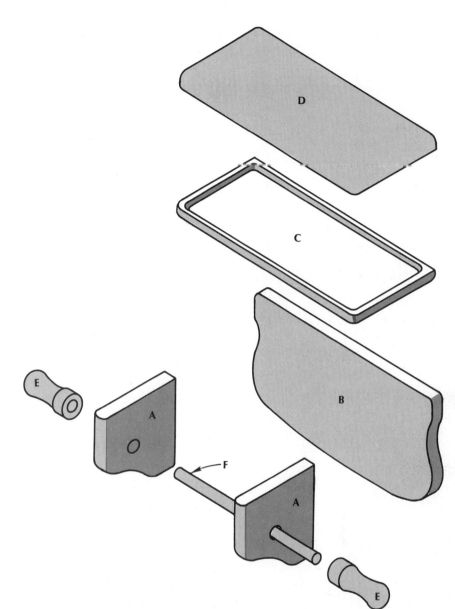

LIST OF MATERIALS

(finished dimensions in inches)

A	Sides (2)	3/4 × 6-1/4 × 6-1/4
B	Back	3/4 × 8-1/2 × 15-1/2
C	Top	3/4 × 7 × 15-1/2
D	Lid	3/4 × 7 × 15-1/2
E	Handles (2)	1-3/4 dia. × 4
F	Towel bar	1 dia. × 14-1/4

KITCHEN ORGANIZER

From *HANDS ON* Sept/Oct 80

Keep all frequently used ingredients and kitchen items within arm's reach. In this clever, compact kitchen organizer, you can store spices, paper towels, tissues, food storage bags, foil, and wrap.

1. Select stock and cut all pieces to size according to the List of Materials. Add an extra 1/2" to the width of the box top to enable you to cut away any splinters caused by edging.

2. Cut all joinery—3/4" × 2-1/2" stop dadoes are cut into the box sides for spice shelves. Cut out the lower contour of the sides (A) with a bandsaw.

3. Drill recesses in the shelves (D) for spice jars with a multi-spur bit or Forstner bit.

4. Drill a pivot hole in the top (B) to start the piercing cut for the tissue dispenser.

5. Cut out the dispenser hole with a jigsaw or sabre saw and sand the inside edge.

6. Edge around the top and inside edge of the dispenser with a router or shaper. Rip the top to width.

7. Turn a cylinder on a lathe to make the towel rod (S).

8. Cut the trough in the marker ledge (J) with a 1" flute molding bit or core box router. Switch to a V-groove cutter and make decorative grooves in the plywood back (F) of the box.

9. Make recesses for hinges in the door frame and sides (A) with a chisel or 1/4" straight router bit.

10. Drill a hole for the door knob.

11. Sand all pieces smooth and complete the assembly.

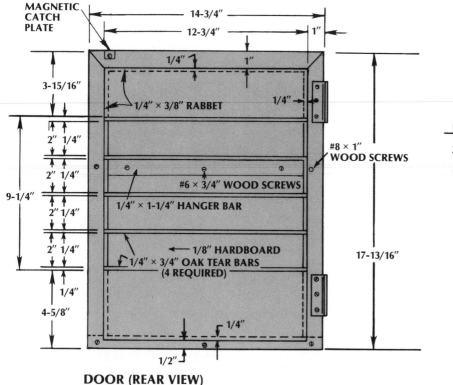

PAPER TOWEL ROD HOLDER

3/4"
2-1/2"
3/4"

DOOR (REAR VIEW)

MAGNETIC CATCH PLATE

14-3/4"
12-3/4"
1"
1/4"
1"
3-15/16"
1/4"
1/4" × 3/8" RABBET
1/4"
2" 1/4"
2" 1/4"
9-1/4"
2" 1/4"
2" 1/4"
1/4"
4-5/8"
1/2"
1/4"

#8 × 1" WOOD SCREWS
#6 × 3/4" WOOD SCREWS
1/4" × 1-1/4" HANGER BAR
1/8" HARDBOARD
1/4" × 3/4" OAK TEAR BARS (4 REQUIRED)
17-13/16"

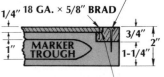

#8 × 1-1/4" FLATHEAD WOOD SCREW
1/4" 18 GA. × 5/8" BRAD
3/4"
MARKER TROUGH
1"
2"
1-1/4"
1/4" WIDE × 3/8" DEEP RABBET

MARKER LEDGE, STILE, AND WRITING BOARD ASSEMBLY

FASTEN HACKSAW BLADE WITH CONTACT CEMENT
1/2"
30°
1/4"
3/4"

OAK TEAR BAR

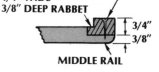

#8 × 1" FLATHEAD WOOD SCREW
1/4" WIDE × 3/8" DEEP RABBET
3/4"
3/8"
MIDDLE RAIL

MIDDLE RAIL AND STILE ASSEMBLY

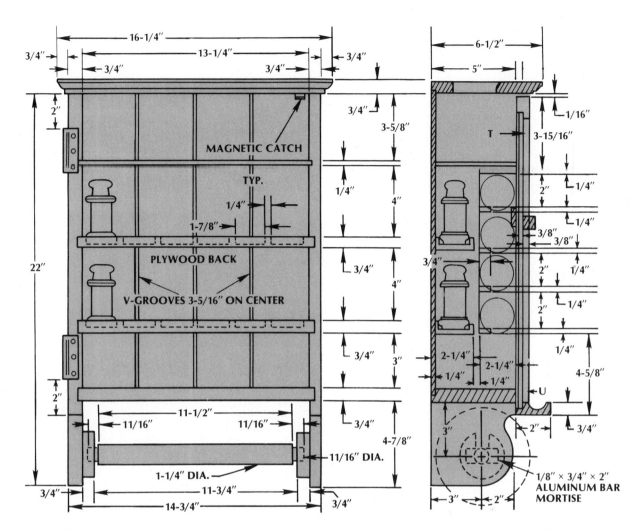

FRONT VIEW — Dimensions: 16-1/4″, 13-1/4″, 3/4″, 3/4″, 3/4″, 2″, 22″, 1/4″, 1-7/8″, 11-1/2″, 11/16″, 11/16″, 11/16″ DIA., 1-1/4″ DIA., 11-3/4″, 14-3/4″, 2″

MAGNETIC CATCH

TYP.

PLYWOOD BACK

V-GROOVES 3-5/16″ ON CENTER

3/4″, 3-5/8″, 1/4″, 4″, 3/4″, 4″, 3/4″, 3″, 3/4″, 4-7/8″

SIDE VIEW — Dimensions: 6-1/2″, 5″, 1/16″, 3-15/16″, 2″, 1/4″, 1/4″, 3/8″, 3/8″, 2″, 1/4″, 1/4″, 4-5/8″, 2-1/4″, 2-1/4″, 1/4″, 1/4″, 2″, 3/4″, 3″, 3″, 2″

T, U

1/8″ × 3/4″ × 2″ ALUMINUM BAR MORTISE

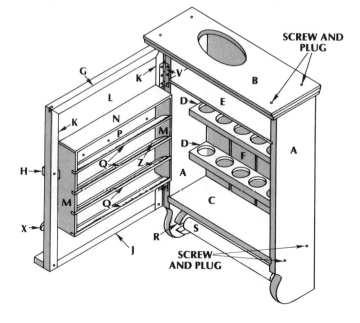

SCREW AND PLUG

SCREW AND PLUG

LIST OF MATERIALS

(finished dimensions in inches)

A	Sides (2)	3/4 × 5 × 22
B	Top	3/4 × 7 × 16-1/4
C	Shelf	3/4 × 5 × 13-3/4
D	Shelves (2)	3/4 × 2-1/4 × 13-3/4
E	Shelf	1/4 × 4-3/4 × 13-3/4
F	Back	1/4 × 13-3/4 × 17-1/8
G	Top rail	3/4 × 1-1/4 × 12-3/4
H	Middle rail	3/4 × 3/4 × 14-3/4
J	Marker ledge	3/4 × 2 × 14-3/4
K	Stiles (2)	3/4 × 1-1/4 × 17-13/16
L	Back	1/8 × 12-3/4 × 16-5/16
M	Sides (2)	1/4 × 2-1/4 × 9
N	Top	1/4 × 2-1/4 × 12-3/4
P	Hanger bar	1/4 × 1-1/4 × 12-1/4
Q	Tear bars (4)	1/4 × 3/4 × 12-3/4
R	Rod holders (2)	3/4 × 2-1/2 × 2-1/2
S	Towel rod	1-1/4 dia. × 12-7/8
T	Cork board	1/16 × 6-1/8 × 12-3/4
U	Writing board	1/8 × 10-3/16 × 12-3/4

51

TAMBOUR BREAD BOX

From *HANDS ON* July/Aug 82

The tambour bread box is a handsome, functional addition to any kitchen. The body is constructed of 3/4" stock and the special tambour door is made from standard screen bead stock. This practical touch helps keep this project easy enough for the beginning woodworker.

1. Cut the stock for the base (A), sides (B), top (C), back (D), front edge (E), and door rail (F), using 3/4" stock. Cut the false back (G) out of 1/4" plywood.

2. Rout the edges on the base (A) and the top (C) with a 3/8" beading bit in a hand router. With a 1/4" router bit, cut the 1/4" deep groove for the false back in both sides (B). Use a router guide.

3. Cut the curves on the sides (B) using the bandsaw.

4. To rout the tambour groove, make a template, according to the drawing, out of 3/8" scrap stock.

Attach it to the side (B). Use a router with a bushing guide and a 3/8" straight bit to rout the groove.

5. Cut the 1/4" deep groove in the top of the tambour door rail (F) using the dado blade. Then cut the tenons on the end of the door rail.

6. Assemble the sides (B), top (C), back (D), front edge (E), and false back (G) together with glue and nails or screws. Cover the heads of the fasteners with putty or plugs.

7. Cut the screen molding (H) to the required length for the tambour door. Glue the strips one by one to the artist's canvas, square the edges, then weight the tambour door down. After the glue has been allowed to set for one hour, remove the weights and bend the door around to ensure against any tambours being stuck together. Glue the first tambour into the groove of the tambour door rail (F). Allow the door assembly to dry for 24 hours.

8. Insert the tambour door into the grooves in the bread box. Check the fit, sanding the edges if needed. Attach the base (A) with wood screws only.

9. Sand the entire project. Attach the knob and apply the finish of your choice.

LIST OF MATERIALS

(finished dimensions in inches)

A	Base	3/4 × 16-1/2 × 19-5/8
B	Sides	3/4 × 11 × 16
C	Top	3/4 × 6-1/4 × 19-1/2
D	Back	3/4 × 11 × 17
E	Front edge	3/4 × 3/4 × 17
F	Door rail	3/4 × 1-3/4 × 17-1/2
G	False back	1/4 × 8 × 17-1/2
H	Screen molding (20)	1/4 × 3/4 × 17-1/2

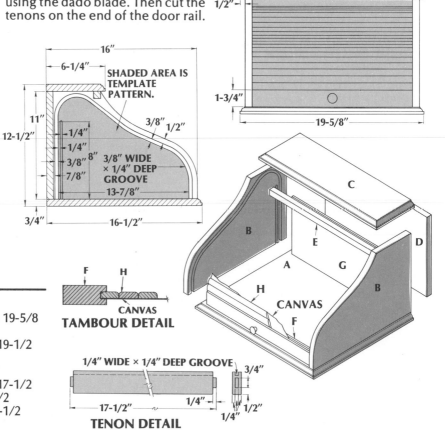

SHADED AREA IS TEMPLATE PATTERN.

3/8" WIDE × 1/4" DEEP GROOVE

TAMBOUR DETAIL

CANVAS

TENON DETAIL

1/4" WIDE × 1/4" DEEP GROOVE

GALLERY RAIL TOWEL HOLDER

From *HANDS ON* July/Aug 82

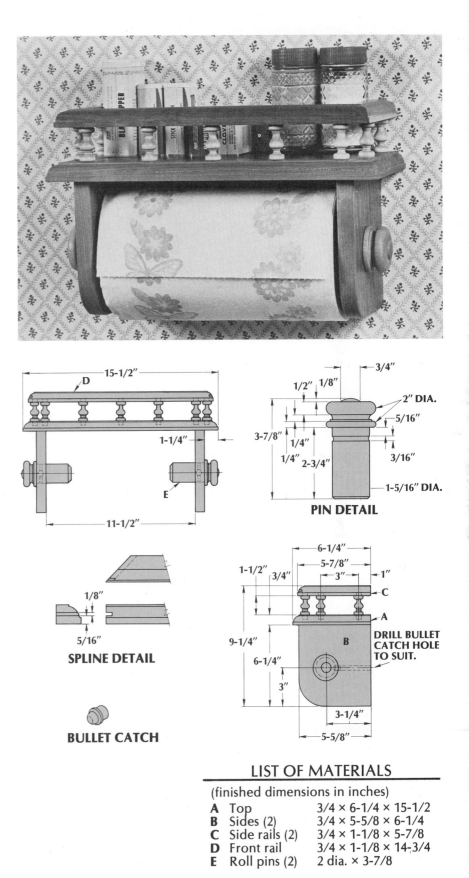

This towel holder turns a plain roll of paper towels into an attractive point of interest in any kitchen. And, it's easier to build than it might look because you make use of gallery spindles that you can buy.

1. Cut the stock for the top (A) and the two sides (B). Cut one piece 3/4″ × 2-1/2″ × 15″ to make the rail parts (C, D).

2. Glue-up the stock for the roll pins (E) using yellow woodworker's glue. Clamp and allow to dry at least 24 hours before turning.

3. Rout or shape the edges of the top (A) and both sides of the 2-1/2″ × 15″ piece. Rip this 2-1/2″ piece into 1-1/8″ wide pieces (C, D).

4. Miter the rail parts (C, D) to size; then, cut the spline grooves. Assemble and clamp the rail together.

5. Drill the holes in sides (B) for the roll pins (E) and the bullet catches. Cut and sand the curves on the two sides (B).

6. Drill the holes in the top (A) and rails for the gallery spindles. Drill and counterbore for screws to assemble the top (A) to the sides (B).

7. Turn the roll pins (E) to shape. Remove the tool rest and sand them while they're still on the lathe.

8. Attach the sides (B) to the top (A), using glue and screws. Plug the screw holes and sand flush. Glue and assemble the gallery pins to the top and the rails.

9. Insert the bullet catches from inside the 1-3/8″ hole, pressing them into place. Friction holds them secure. Apply the finish of your choice.

PIN DETAIL

SPLINE DETAIL

BULLET CATCH

DRILL BULLET CATCH HOLE TO SUIT.

LIST OF MATERIALS

(finished dimensions in inches)

A	Top	3/4 × 6-1/4 × 15-1/2
B	Sides (2)	3/4 × 5-5/8 × 6-1/4
C	Side rails (2)	3/4 × 1-1/8 × 5-7/8
D	Front rail	3/4 × 1-1/8 × 14-3/4
E	Roll pins (2)	2 dia. × 3-7/8

KITCHEN SLIDE RULE

From *HANDS ON* Nov/Dec 83

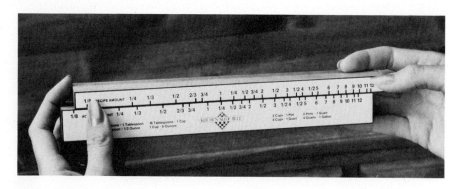

This slide rule is a handy tool that allows the cook to alter recipes for more or fewer people. It also comes in handy when you need to adjust a recipe because you have a limited supply of one ingredient on hand—two eggs instead of three, for instance.

This easy-to-make slide rule is a router attachment project. We've included the full-sized scale that you can photocopy. The slide rule is 10" long. You can easily perform the same operations on 41" long stock and make four of these calculators at one time.

Prepare enough 1" × 1-1/2" clear stock for the number of slide rules you make. Joint or sand the edges smooth. Prepare matching scrap pieces for test cuts.

Now use the drill press. Mount the router chuck with a 1/4" straight router bit and cut a 1/2" deep groove in the center of the bottom half of the stock. Use feather boards and a push stick. Switch to the dovetail router bit and rout out the dovetail slot. Next, rout the dovetail tongue. Set the machine so you are cutting with the stock between the bit and fence and feed the stock from right to left against the rotation.

Check the fit of the slide. If it's too loose, insert a bullet catch (available at most hardware stores) to provide the tension you need.

Finally, glue on the scale and apply varnish. Wax the dovetail slot with a good quality furniture paste wax.

To use the rule, set the amount the recipe calls for on the top scale over the amount you want on the bottom scale. For example, if the recipe serves eight and you need to fix enough for ten, set the eight over the ten. Now, as you read the recipe, locate the quantity your recipe calls for on the upper scale and read the actual amount you need directly below it on the lower scale.

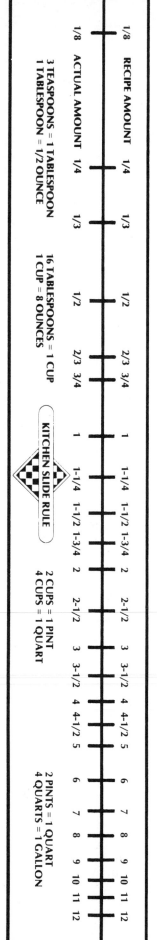

1-1/2"

1-1/2"

10"

10"

1/4"   1/2" 1"

1/2"

1/2" 1"

5/16"

9/16"

**BULLET CATCH
PROVIDES TENSION
(OPTIONAL)**

TURNING A WOODEN PLACE SETTING

From *HANDS ON* Nov/Dec 80

For most of us, it was our first woodturning project—turning a bowl on a lathe. But afterward we went on to bigger and better things and forgot about that simple bowl that once had us basking in the glory of our own accomplishment.

However, turning wooden utensils is more than just an educational exercise. Few woodworkers have mastered it; most of us are still trying and learning. But with just a little bit of practice, you can do simple, beautiful bowls, plates, and goblets.

THE MATERIALS

Kitchen and dining utensils have to stand up under a lot of abuse. Bowls and plates are constantly banged and scraped with forks and spoons. Soup bowls and goblets have to hold both hot and cold liquids. And all utensils need to be washed again and again.

In general, close-grained hardwoods make more serviceable goblets, bowls, and plates than softwoods. They resist indentation and the density of the wood helps to repel moisture.

Oily woods do better than those with few natural oils. Teak and rosewood are permeated with oils that prevent them from absorbing moisture. With other woods, it's advisable to apply a lavish coat of waterproof finish and hope that it soaks in. But this soaking is at best an imperfect substitute for a wood's own natural, waterproofing oils.

In considering what materials to turn, you may have to make some tradeoffs. Cherry, for example, doesn't have the natural oils that rosewood has, but it's easier to find and a lot less expensive. Cedar, although it's not a hardwood, is inexpensive, loaded with oils, and will not absorb odors from the foods that come in contact with it.

LAMINATING RINGS

When you turned that first bowl, you probably used a solid laminated block of wood. And you scraped and scraped and scraped and scraped until the center was hollowed out and the sides were sloped. There is, however, an easier and more economical way to turn bowls and plates without wasting all that time and wood.

It involves stacking overlapping concentric rings. These rings are cut with either a bandsaw or jigsaw from a single piece of wood. After cutting, these rings are stacked in a cone shape. Turning is faster because the shape of the object is partially formed.

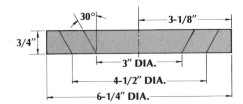
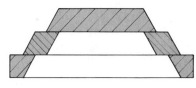

The rings needed to turn a bowl can be cut from a single board and glued and stacked.

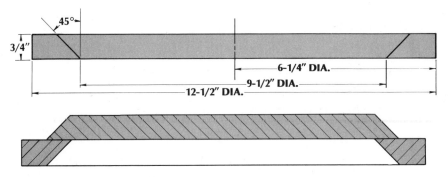

When making a bowl or plate, cuts are made, then stacked and glued to form general shape.

(continues on next page)

To cut out these concentric rings, use a compass to mark several circles on top of the board used. The circles will be cut out at an angle that is determined by the shape you want your finished turning to have and the slope of its sides.

If you use a jigsaw, you'll have to drill several 1/8" pilot holes to start the cuts. Be sure these holes are drilled at the same angle as the cuts you're about to make. Tilt the jigsaw table at the desired angle, slip a 1/8" blade through a pilot hole, and cut. Repeat until you have separated all the rings.

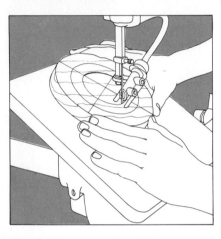

Cut the rings at a 30° angle on a jigsaw.

If you use a bandsaw, split the board down the middle instead of making pilot holes. Cut out each half-ring with the bandsaw table tilted at the proper angle. Glue these rings back together with waterproof glue.

Stack the rings one on top of the other and glue them together with waterproof resorcinol glue. If you're working with a dense, oily

wood like rosewood or teak, wipe the gluing surface with paint thinner before applying the glue to get a better bond.

Be sure, after you've stacked the rings, that all the grains run in the same direction. Laminating the

grains perpendicular to each other will in some cases increase the strength of a piece; but in this case, it will also increase the likelihood of splitting out. Wood expands up to ten times as much across the grain as with the grain when it

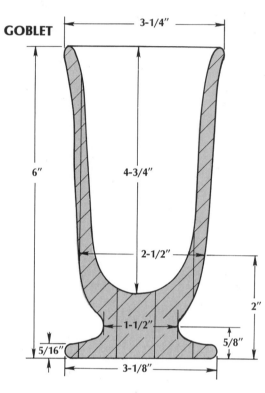

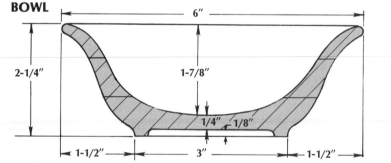

comes in contact with moisture. By running all the grains in the same direction, you insure that the laminations don't fight each other. Allow laminations to remain clamped for at least 24 hours before turning.

MOUNTING

To properly turn bowls and plates, you need to mount your stock on a faceplate twice. The first mounting allows you to turn the outside and the base of the utensil; with the second mounting, you turn the inside.

Select the proper size faceplate or screw mount and attach a mounting block to it. This block should be solid wood with no cracks or checks. Center the mounting block and glue it in place with aliphatic resin and a paper spacer between the mounting block and the turning stock. Allow the glue to dry overnight before turning. When dry, turn the outside of the bowl to the desired shape.

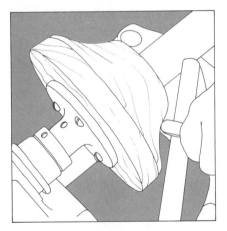

Turn the outside of the bowl.

Separate the turning from the block by carefully wedging them apart with a chisel. The paper spacer will insure that they come apart cleanly and easily, without tearing wood away from the turning stock.

Replace the mounting block with another that will fit inside the turned base, glue it to the stock as before. Turn the inside of the piece, separate it from the mount, and clean off the glue with a chisel and a little water.

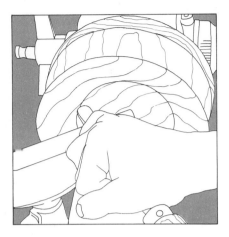

Turn the inside of the bowl.

TURNING A BOWL AND PLATE

The bowl and plate are each made from a single piece of 3/4" thick stock; the piece used to form the bowl is 6-1/2" square; and the one used to form the plate is 12-1/2" square.

To make the rings for the bowl, draw three concentric circles on the stock 3", 4-1/2", and 6-1/4" in diameter. Cut these on a 30° angle from vertical.

To make the rings for the plate, draw two concentric circles 9-1/2" and 12-1/2" in diameter, and cut on a 45° angle.

Laminate the rings, mount the turning stock, and turn the outside and inside contours.

TURNING A GOBLET

Unlike the bowl and plate, the best way to turn a goblet or utensil with nearly vertical sides is to use a solid block of wood. Cut or laminate a block 6" high and 3-3/4" on a side. Mount this using either the screw center or small faceplate.

Turn the outside of the goblet as if you were doing spindle turning, using the tailstock and dead center. After you've shaped the outside, remove the dead center from the tailstock and replace it with the chuck arbor. Mount the drill chuck on the chuck arbor, and a 1-3/4" drill bit in the chuck. With the drill

bit stationary and the workpiece turning, use the quill to drill out most of the inside contour of the goblet. Afterward, finish turning the inside as you did the bowl and plate.

PAD FINISHING

After sanding the workpiece smooth, keep it turning. Dip a #00 steel wool pad in a nontoxic finish such as mineral oil or salad bowl finish. Apply the finish evenly and liberally to the surface of the utensil as it turns. Squeeze the pad gently to achieve a uniform flow of finish onto the wood. Keep the wood wet for at least 5 minutes, giving the finish a chance to soak in.

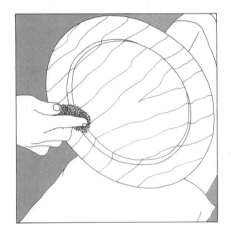

Pad finish the plate.

Apply at least two coats of finish; you can apply the second one a little more sparingly than the first. As the wood turns, the fine steel wool will buff the finish to a soft luster. Separate the piece from the mount, scrape away the glue, and apply a coat to the area where the mount mates to the utensil.

By keeping several turnings going at once, turning one while the glue on another cures and the finish on a third dries, you can turn four or more place settings in a few days. Your new place setting may not have the sentimental value of your first bowl, but you can be just as proud.

COLONIAL SPICE CABINET

From *HANDS ON* Jan/Feb/Mar 83

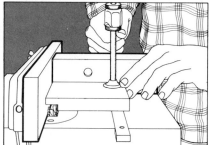

Use an auxiliary fence and a miter gauge extension to make cutting rabbets in the drawer fronts easier and safer.

This charming project is made from 1/2", 3/8", and 1/4" pine or hardwood stock that you can prepare on the bandsaw and/or thickness planer.

1. Resaw a 5' piece of 1 × 4 stock on the bandsaw for the 1/4" and 3/8" pieces. Use the miter gauge with a wooden fence extension and set up the cut so you will end up with 9/32" and 13/32" thick boards. Cutting the stock a little oversize gives you room to sand or plane it to proper thickness.

2. Prepare a 4' length of 1 × 10 and a 7' piece of 1 × 4 to 1/2" thickness.

3. Cut the back (B) from the wide stock. Then rip the 1/4" stock to 3-1/8" for the drawer backs (K, L) and bottoms (M, N). Rip the sides (A) to 4". Do not rip the back to finished width yet.

4. Cut to length all remaining parts according to the List of Materials. Tip: Cut the long stock into manageable pieces; then, use a stop block on the fence.

5. Form the rabbets in the backs of the sides (A) with the dado accessory. Use the fence shown in *Power Tool Woodworking for Everyone* for this operation. Next, cut the rabbets in the drawer fronts (G, H) using the same fence attachment and a miter gauge extension for support. Cut dadoes in the sides (A) and partitions (C, F).

6. Cut the grooves for drawer bottoms in the drawer sides (J) and the drawer fronts (G, H) with the dado accessory.

7. Cut out the contours on the sides (A). Use the bandsaw or jigsaw.

8. Dry-assemble the sides (A) and parts (C, D, E, F) with clamps and check for fit. Disassemble and then use glue and 4d finishing nails on the outside joints. Use glue only on the interior joints.

9. Rip the back (B) to width, then cut and sand the top and bottom contours. Drill the 1/4" mounting hole then attach the back with 1" brads.

10. Drill the knob mounting holes in the drawer fronts (G, H).

11. Assemble the drawers with glue and 3/4" brads. After the glue has dried, sand each drawer to fit. Use

LIST OF MATERIALS

(finished dimensions in inches)

A	Sides (2)	1/2 × 4 × 20
B	Back	1/2 × 8-1/2 × 24-3/4
C	Horizontal partitions (2)	1/2 × 3-1/2 × 8-1/4
D	Bottom	1/2 × 3-1/2 × 8-1/4
E	Drawer partitions (4)	1/2 × 3-1/2 × 4
F	Vertical partition	1/2 × 3-1/2 × 11-3/4
G	Small drawer fronts (6)	1/2 × 3-1/2 × 3-3/4
H	Large drawer front	1/2 × 3-1/2 × 8
J	Drawer sides (14)	3/8 × 3-1/2 × 3-1/4
K	Small drawer backs (6)	1/4 × 3-1/8 × 3
L	Large drawer back	1/4 × 3-1/8 × 7-1/4
M	Small drawer bottoms (6)	1/4 × 3-1/8 × 3-1/4
N	Large drawer bottom	1/4 × 3-1/8 × 7-1/2

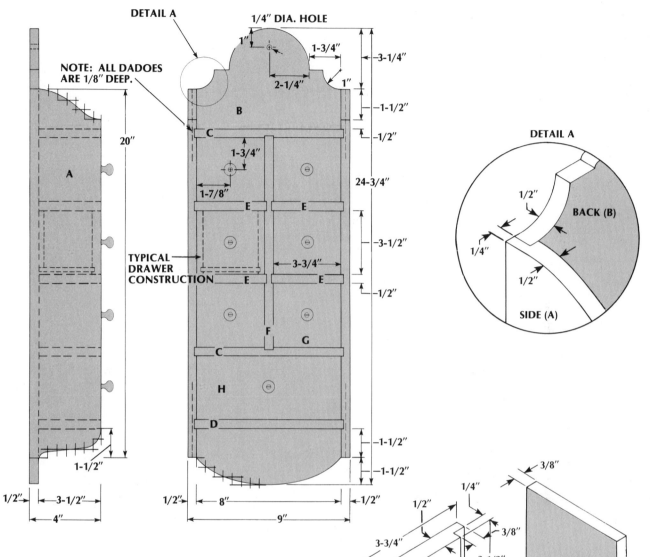

DETAIL A

1/4" DIA. HOLE

NOTE: ALL DADOES ARE 1/8" DEEP.

1"

1-3/4"

3-1/4"

2-1/4"

1"

B

20"

C

1-3/4"

1-1/2"

1/2"

A

1-7/8"

24-3/4"

TYPICAL DRAWER CONSTRUCTION

E   E

3-1/2"

3-3/4"

E   E

1/2"

F

G

C

H

D

1-1/2"

1-1/2"

1/2"   3-1/2"   1/2"   8"   1/2"
4"   9"

DETAIL A

1/2"

BACK (B)

1/4"

1/2"

SIDE (A)

a disc or belt sander. Number the drawers on the back for location.
12. Finish sand the entire cabinet and round all edges slightly for a well-worn, colonial effect. Apply stain, if desired, and finish. Attach drawer knobs.

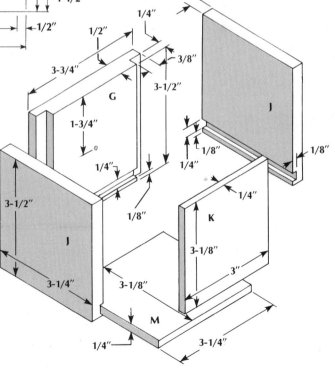

3/8"

1/4"

1/2"

3-3/4"

G

3/8"

3-1/2"

1-3/4"

J

1/4"

1/8"

1/8"

1/4"

1/4"

3-1/2"

1/8"

J

K

1/4"

3-1/8"

3-1/2"

3"

3-1/4"

3-1/8"

M

1/4"

3-1/4"

UTENSIL RACK

From *HANDS ON* Nov/Dec 80

Most modern kitchens are small, so space must be used efficiently. A good addition to any kitchen is a utensil rack where you can hang pots, pans, and other cooking utensils.

1. Cut all pieces to size, according to the List of Materials. Use the table saw.

2. Drill 3/4" dowel holes in the ends of the rails (A). Set up the rip fence and miter gauge to speed the process and provide accuracy.

3. Drill the 3/8" holes for the pegs (C) in two of the rails. Tilt the table 15° and determine the spacing for the holes.

4. Pad drill 3/4" dowel holes in the battens (B). Pad drilling the battens assures accurate alignment of the holes.

5. Assemble the rack by gluing the rails (A) to the battens (B) and inserting the dowels (D). After the glue has dried, sand the front of the rack flush. Next glue the pegs (C) into place.

6. Attach the plexiglass (E) to the back of the battens with #8 × 3/4" flathead wood screws. Drill countersinks in the plexiglass so the screws will be flush with the surface. The plexiglass protects the wall from hanging pots.

7. Finish the rack using polyurethane or any other water-resistant finish. Attach the rack to the wall, then make pan hooks from 1/8" diameter steel rod. Use pliers to form square corners and form the curve around 1" diameter pipe.

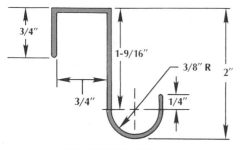

HOOK DETAIL

LIST OF MATERIALS

(finished dimensions in inches)

A	Rails (9)	3/4 × 2 × 24
B	Battens (2)	3/4 × 1-1/2 × 24
C	Pegs (10)	3/8 dia. × 3
D	Dowels (18)	3/4 dia. × 1-1/2
E	Plexiglass	1/8 × 18 × 24

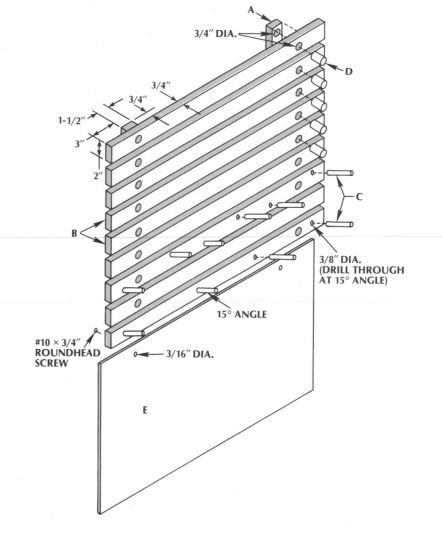

From *HANDS ON* Mar/Apr/May 84

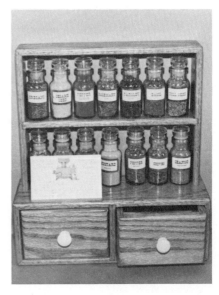

Cooks appreciate this attractive piece that organizes their recipes and spices in a neat, compact unit.

1. Prepare stock by using the bandsaw and/or thickness planer. Select good clear stock that's straight and free of defects.

2. Cut the stock to size according to the List of Materials. Rip all stock to the correct width then crosscut to correct lengths. When crosscutting, leave a little extra stock on the shelf (C), partition (F), and the drawer parts (G, H, J, K). Disc sand or cut these to final length later.

3. Cut the 45° miters on parts (A, B, D, E).

4. Cut the dadoes and rabbets in all parts. Next, cut the 1/8" groove in the drawer parts (G, H, J) for the drawer bottoms (K). Then cut the 1/8" wide × 1/4" deep groove in the top (D) of the drawer case to hold recipe cards.

5. Dry-assemble the drawer case and upper frame. Measure for the finished lengths of shelf (C) and partition (F) then cut or disc sand to length. Glue and clamp parts (A, B, C). Attach (D) to this assembly with #8 × 1-1/4" flathead wood screws and glue. Glue and clamp the remaining drawer case parts (D, E, F) to the upper frame assembly. Attach the drawer unit back (L) with brads.

6. Assemble the drawers with glue and clamps. Sand the drawers on the disc sander until they fit with the case.

Locate and drill the mounting holes for the drawer knobs.

7. Round the edges of the drawer fronts and the front edges of the case. Use a handheld router and a 1/4" quarter round bit, or use a rasp and sandpaper. Sand the project thoroughly and apply the finish of your choice.

LIST OF MATERIALS

(finished dimensions in inches)

A	Shelf sides (2)	1/2 × 2-1/2 × 10
B	Top	1/2 × 2-1/2 × 13
C	Shelf	1/2 × 2-1/2 × 12-1/2
D	Drawer case top and bottom (2)	1/2 × 5 × 14
E	Drawer case sides (2)	1/2 × 5 × 4-3/4
F	Drawer case partition	1/2 × 4-3/4 × 4-1/4
G	Drawer fronts (2)	1/2 × 3-3/4 × 6-1/4
H	Drawer backs (2)	1/2 × 3-3/4 × 5-3/4
J	Drawer sides (4)	1/2 × 3-3/4 × 4-1/2
K	Drawer bottoms (2)	1/8 × 3-3/4 × 5-1/2
L	Drawer unit back	1/4 × 4-1/4 × 13-1/2

CASE ASSEMBLY

1/2" WIDE × 1/4" DEEP DADO
1/8" WIDE × 1/8" DEEP GROOVE (ALL FOUR SIDES)
1/4"
J
H
K
3-1/8"
1-7/8"
G
1/2" WIDE × 1/4" DEEP RABBET
J
1/8"

DRAWER ASSEMBLY

5"
4-1/2"
A
B
C
45° MITER
1/8" WIDE × 1/4" DEEP GROOVE
1/2" WIDE × 1/4" DEEP DADO
1/2" WIDE × 1/4" DEEP DADO
A
D
1/4" WIDE × 1/4" DEEP RABBET ON UNDERSIDE FOR DRAWER UNIT BACK (L)
1/4" WIDE × 1/4" DEEP RABBET
E
F
L
D
L
1/2" WIDE × 1/4" DEEP DADO
6-3/4"
1/4" WIDE × 1/4" DEEP RABBET

HOT POT TILE

From *HANDS ON* Sept/Oct 83

Here's a trivet that solves the problem of where to set hot dishes in the kitchen. First, select decorative tiles from a building supply or flooring outlet store. Cut 1/2" or 3/4" plywood the same size as the tile. Make the molding on the shaper or the molder and cut to size. (Thickness of the molding will depend on thickness of the plywood and the tile.)

Assemble the trivet by applying mastic to the bottom of the tile and one side of the plywood. Next, apply mastic to the edges and the molding and attach the molding. Mastic acts as a filler and an adhesive so there's no need to clamp. Set the project on a piece of waxed paper and allow to dry at least 24 hours.

Clean off excess mastic around the tile with mineral spirits and use the belt sander to remove excess mastic from the bottom of the trivet.

Finally, apply the stain or finish of your choice. Screw rubber feet on to the base as a final touch.

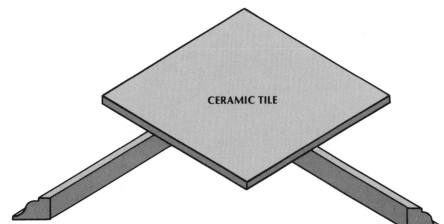

CERAMIC TILE

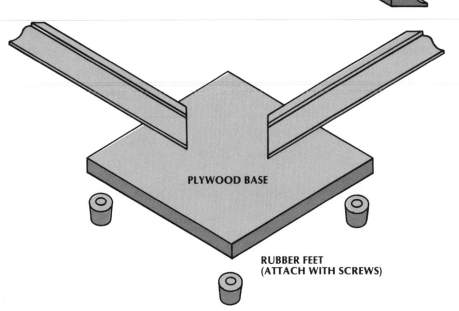

PLYWOOD BASE

RUBBER FEET
(ATTACH WITH SCREWS)

From *HANDS ON* Sept/Oct 83

This project protects fingers from getting burned when removing hot items from the toaster. Select a suitable hardwood such as maple, cherry, or walnut. Cut the stock into 3/4″ × 7/8″ × 6-1/4″ pieces. Drill the 5/8″ hole in the 7/8″ side of the stock. Next, cut out the excess stock with a bandsaw or jigsaw. Using the disc sander, sand off any saw marks and bevel the tips of the tongs. Finish with a non-toxic finish such as salad bowl finish or mineral oil.

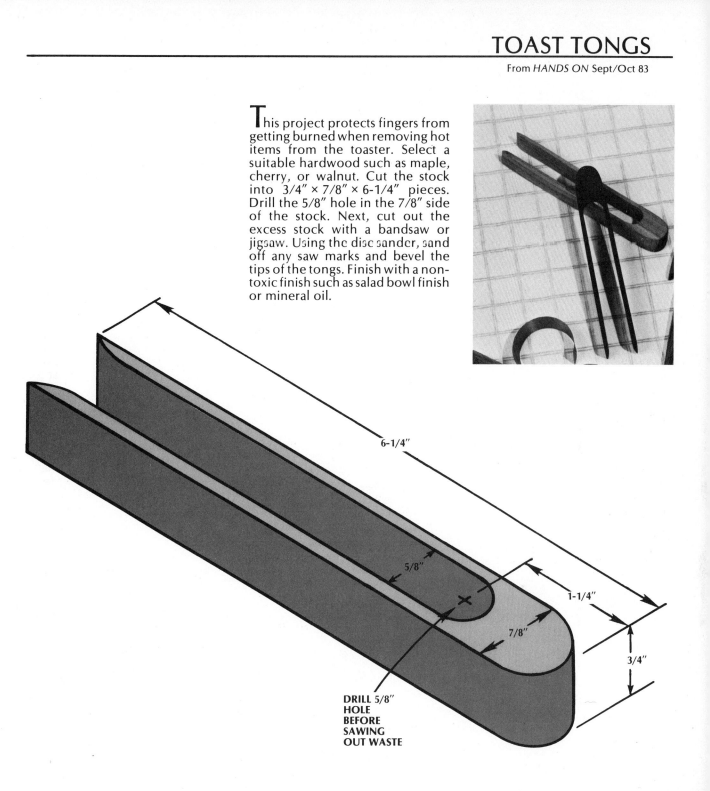

6-1/4″

5/8″

1-1/4″

7/8″

3/4″

**DRILL 5/8″
HOLE
BEFORE
SAWING
OUT WASTE**

Toys

Here are seventeen easy-to-build toys that will not only be a joy to make, but will also please the little ones in your life. Toys should be built with the child in mind, so there's always the need for safety. When making toys, be sure to avoid any sharp edges or corners; sand all parts of a project well to eliminate any chance of splinters; glue and clamp all parts securely and reinforce larger parts with dowels or screws; and, finally, use only nontoxic finishes.

ROCKING HORSE

From *HANDS ON* Sept/Oct 83

Design copyright © 1983 Robert Lee

used to align the various parts of the body during assembly. (Drill the 1" deep alignment holes for the legs [B, C] from the back without drilling through the stock.)

3. Sand all contoured parts on the disc and drum sanders. To ensure that the rockers (A) are identical, tape them together with double-faced carpet tape so they can be pad sanded.

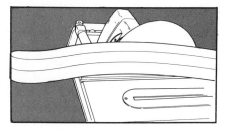

The rockers are sanded to identical contours by pad sanding.

4. Use the shaper with a groove cutter and shape a 1/4" deep groove in the back of the head (E) for the mane.

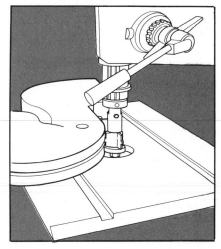

Cut the groove in the back of the head with the groove cutter.

Making a toy for a child is fun. Hours spent cutting, sanding, and finishing a toy are richly rewarded with the happiness shown on a child's face when he or she receives it. A very popular toy that woodworkers have made to delight children over the years is the rocking horse. Now you can make this favorite toy and please a child by using the easy-to-follow plans provided below. This simple design can be completed by the average woodworker in under 12 hours and costs less than $30 for materials.

1. Use the drawings provided to make full-scale patterns of parts (A-H). First draw a 1" grid on cardboard or hardboard; then, transfer the drawings to the grid. Next, cut out the pattern and transfer it to a 6' and 8' length of 2 × 12 stock.

Work around any knots or defects and, for maximum strength, make sure you follow the grain direction noted by arrows.

Cut the stock into manageable pieces before attempting to cut out the final shapes on the bandsaw or jigsaw. The saddle (G) can be made out of 2 × 12 stock and shaped, or made from 3/4" stock (H) and upholstered (see step 11). Cut the braces (J) to size and chamfer the edges on the table saw (see *Power Tool Woodworking for Everyone*). Or you can use the disc sander to chamfer the ends of the braces.

2. Drill the holes for the handle, eyes, and tail where noted in the drawings. Drill the alignment holes in parts (B, C, D, E, F). Locate these holes very carefully since they are

5. Mark the outside edges of parts (B, C, D, E, G) and round them on the shaper using a 1/4" quarter round cutter or a router using a round over bit. Do not round the neck where it meets with the body since these edges must be square.

66

6. Assemble the main body parts (D, E, F). Use dowel rods to align the parts when gluing and clamping, but do not glue the dowels in place yet. The body can also be assembled with #10 × 2-1/2″ flathead wood screws. Sand the body assembly on the disc sander so all the parts are flush.

7. Mount the legs (B, C). Align the legs with 3/8″ dowel rods that extend through the body and into the legs on both sides. Disassemble and then glue and clamp the legs into place with the dowel rods.

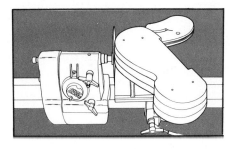

Sand the assembled body contour flush on the disc sander.

You can also assemble the legs without the glue and just use #10 × 2-1/2″ flathead wood screws. This permits the final project to be disassembled for shipping or storing. The screws can be covered with stain or paint later.

8. Center the braces (J) on the feet and attach with #10 × 1-1/2″ flathead wood screws. Then, place the horse with the attached braces on the rockers. Make sure the horse is sitting level on the rockers by sliding it back and forth until the body is parallel to the floor. Fasten with #10 × 1-1/2″ flathead wood screws.

Attach the remaining braces (J) with #10 × 1-1/2″ flathead wood screws. Round off the hard edges of the rockers at this point. (The rockers need to remain fairly square for stability.)

(continues on next page)

3/8″ DIA. ×
1″ DEEP HOLE
(2 REQUIRED)

LIST OF MATERIALS

(finished dimensions in inches)

A	Rockers (2)	1-1/2 × 7 × 40-3/4
B	Front legs (2)	1-1/2 × 5-5/8 × 19-1/8
C	Rear legs (2)	1-1/2 × 7-1/8 × 20-1/4
D	Sides (2)	1-1/2 × 9 × 21-3/8
E	Head	1-1/2 × 11 × 19-1/4
F	Rear body	1-1/2 × 8-3/4 × 13-3/4
G	Saddle	1-1/2 × 10-1/2 × 8-1/2
H	Saddle (optional)	3/4 × 10-1/2 × 8-1/2
J	Braces (5)	3/4 × 3-1/2 × 14
K	Handle	3/4 dia. × 9

9. Attach the saddle (G or H). The backup board for the upholstered saddle (H) is attached with #10 × 1-1/2" flathead wood screws. The solid wood saddle (G) is attached with 3/8" dowels and glue. Drill three 3/8" dowels in the bottom of the seat and locate matching dowel holes on the body. Drill these holes with a hand drill and attach the seat with glue. Use a weight on the seat or use a web clamp for clamping.

10. Apply the stain and finish of your choice. For this project one coat of stain and two coats of polyurethane varnish were used.

11. (Optional) Upholster the saddle (H). Cut out and chamfer the top edges of 2" thick foam rubber on the bandsaw. Then, cut the saddle covering out of cloth, vinyl, or leather. Attach the front edge of the material to the front of the backup board. Pull material back over the foam. Locate the back

edge and insert an upholstery tack strip (available from upholstery shops) through the material. Fold the tack strip under the foam and pound the tacks in by hitting the seat with a rubber mallet. Tack the sides of the covering under the saddle and along the sides. Pleat the material as you go by folding it under and securing it with upholstery tacks or staples.

12. To make the horse's mane, use a skein of rug yarn and unloop it. Cut it into three equal parts (about 14" lengths). Next, take a piece of 1/2" wide durable tape (reinforced, duct, etc.) and lay it out on a flat surface with the sticky side up. Lay the yarn across the tape and press it down to secure it. (For additional strength, stitch the yarn onto the tape with a sewing machine.) After the yarn is secured to the tape, glue the mane into the head groove. Use a small stick to force it into the

groove. (Several small pieces of wood can be used as wedges to hold the mane in place while the glue dries.)

13. The tail is made from a single skein of rug yarn, unlooped and cut. Wrap 2" of one end of this yarn with a section of yarn and tie securely. This will help the tail stand out from the body. Glue the tail into place.

14. The eyes can be found at most craft shops. The eyes on this project have 1/4" stems and are glued into place with aliphatic resin (yellow) glue. Or, you can simply paint the eyes on.

15. To make the ears, cut four triangles out of soft leather or vinyl. Put two triangles face-to-face and stitch where indicated in the drawing. Turn these inside out, fold the bottom corners together, and attach to the horse's head with small screws.

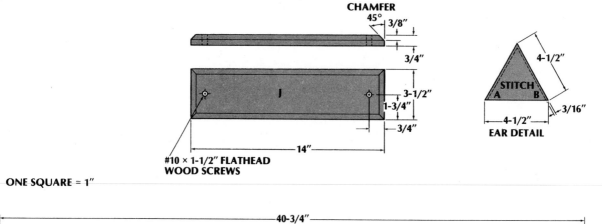

ONE SQUARE = 1"

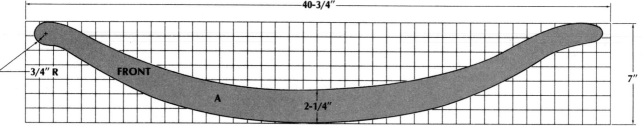

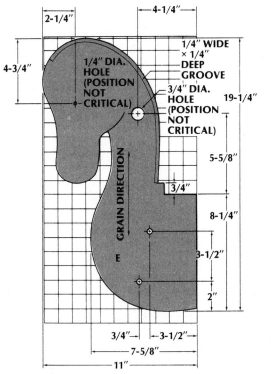

2-1/4"
4-1/4"
1/4" WIDE × 1/4" DEEP GROOVE
1/4" DIA. HOLE (POSITION NOT CRITICAL)
3/4" DIA. HOLE (POSITION NOT CRITICAL)
4-3/4"
19-1/4"
GRAIN DIRECTION
3/4"
5-5/8"
8-1/4"
3-1/2"
2"
E
3/4"
3-1/2"
7-5/8"
11"

ONE SQUARE = 1"

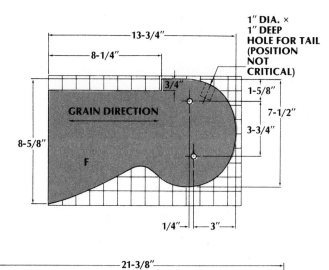

1" DIA. × 1" DEEP HOLE FOR TAIL (POSITION NOT CRITICAL)
13-3/4"
8-1/4"
3/4"
1-5/8"
7-1/2"
3-3/4"
GRAIN DIRECTION
8-5/8"
F
1/4"
3"

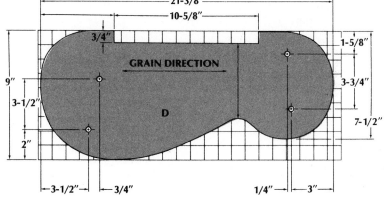

21-3/8"
10-5/8"
3/4"
1-5/8"
GRAIN DIRECTION
9"
3-3/4"
D
3-1/2"
7-1/2"
2"
3-1/2"
3/4"
1/4"
3"

TIP: MAKE PATTERN FOR PART (D) FIRST AND TRANSFER HOLE ALIGNMENT POSITIONS TO OTHER PARTS.

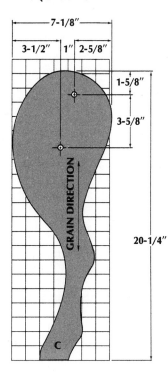

7-1/8"
3-1/2"
1"
2-5/8"
1-5/8"
3-5/8"
GRAIN DIRECTION
20-1/4"
C

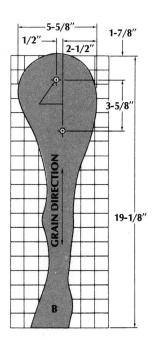

5-5/8"
1-7/8"
1/2"
2-1/2"
3-5/8"
GRAIN DIRECTION
19-1/8"
B

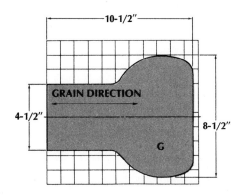

10-1/2"
GRAIN DIRECTION
4-1/2"
8-1/2"
G

69

From *HANDS ON* Sept/Oct 81

To craft your own toy trolley, start by making the two pieces (E, F) that form the roof.

1. Cut all stock according to the List of Materials.

2. Tilt the saw to 12° and use a hollow-ground blade to cut a bevel around the outside edges of the roof (E, F).

3. Using a dado blade, rabbet the underside of both roof sections. Use a bandsaw to cut the curved undercarriage (H). Cut and shape the observation rails (B).

4. Drill holes as indicated on the patterns. Drill the axle holes in the undercarriage (H) using the horizontal boring mode. Change to the drill press mode and drill matched holes in the lower roof (E) and the trolley body (C) for roof supports.

5. Cut the wheels out using a jigsaw, bandsaw, or 1-1/2" hole saw. If you use a hole saw, you can eliminate the splintering that occurs as you pierce the wood if you stop the hole saw just as the pilot drill pierces the underside of the workpiece. Then, turn the piece over and finish the hole. Use a backup block to protect the worktable. Finish sand the wheels as round as possible. Use hardwood for the axles and wheels. As children play with toys, these pieces take a lot of abuse. Cut axles from a dowel rod and rub them with paraffin for smooth operation.

6. Assemble all pieces with aliphatic resin (yellow) glue.

7. In crafting toys, you must build safety into each piece. Sand with extra-fine sandpaper to eliminate splinters and sharp edges. Use a nontoxic product to finish your project such as mineral oil or salad bowl finish.

LIST OF MATERIALS

(finished dimensions in inches)

A	Base	3/16 × 2-7/8 × 10-1/2
B	Observation rails (2)	5/16 × 2-7/8 × 1-3/16
C	Body	1 × 2-1/4 × 8-3/4
D	Roof supports (14)	1/4 dia. × 2
E	Lower roof	3/4 × 3-5/8 × 11-1/8
F	Upper roof	1 × 2-1/4 × 10-1/2
G	Steps (2)	1/2 × 1/2 × 4-3/4
H	Undercarriage	1-1/8 × 1-7/8 × 8-3/4
J	Axles (2)	1/4 dia. × 2-7/8
K	Wheels (4)	1-3/8 dia. × 3/8

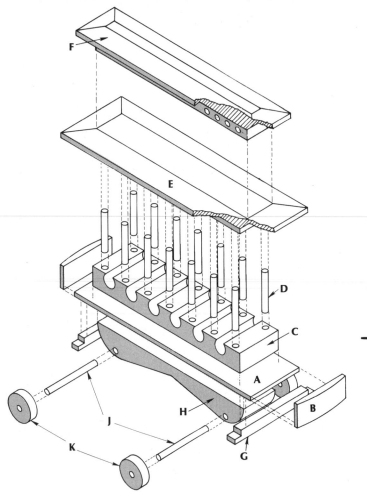

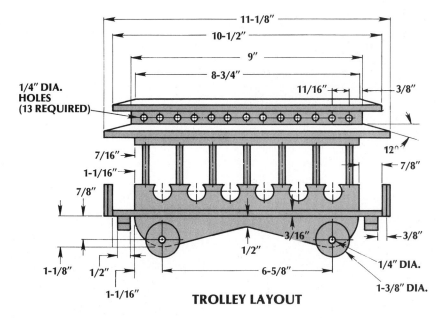

1/4" DIA. HOLES (13 REQUIRED)

11-1/8"
10-1/2"
9"
8-3/4"
11/16"
3/8"
7/16"
1-1/16"
7/8"
7/8"
12°
1-1/8"
1/2"
1-1/16"
1/2"
3/16"
6-5/8"
3/8"
1/4" DIA.
1-3/8" DIA.

TROLLEY LAYOUT

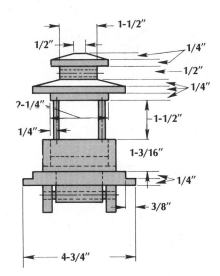

1/2"
1-1/2"
1/4"
1/2"
1/4"
2-1/4"
1/4"
1-1/2"
1/4"
1-3/16"
1/4"
3/8"
4-3/4"

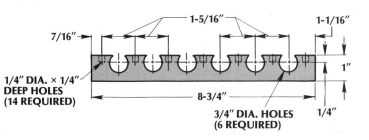

7/16"
1-5/16"
1-1/16"
1/4" DIA. × 1/4"
DEEP HOLES
(14 REQUIRED)
8-3/4"
3/4" DIA. HOLES
(6 REQUIRED)
1"
1/4"

BODY DETAIL

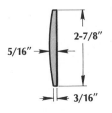

OBSERVATION RAIL DETAIL

2-7/8"
5/16"
3/16"

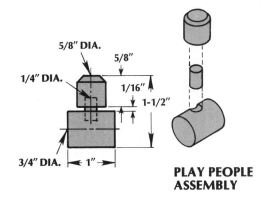

5/8" DIA.
5/8"
1/4" DIA.
1/16"
1-1/2"
3/4" DIA.
1"

PLAY PEOPLE ASSEMBLY

From *HANDS ON* Nov/Dec 79

Children have a particular fascination for flight. The first toy airplane was manufactured years before the first airplane had ever flown. Here's a biplane, a design that has intrigued pilots (and future pilots) since the first days of powered flight.

1. Cut all pieces to size and shape, using the patterns provided and List of Materials. Drill a 7/16" axle hole in each of the landing struts (L), with the center of the hole 1/2" from one end of the strut. Drill a 7/16" hole in the center of the propeller (H) and 3/8" holes in the center of the wheels (N) and keeper (K). Drill four 3/8" holes at a 15° angle in the top wing (D) and bottom wing (E). Centers of the wing holes should be 3" from the wing tips and 3/4" from the leading and trailing edges, as shown on the pattern. Drill two 1" holes in the bottom wing (E). The centers of these holes should be 1-1/8" from the center of the wing and 1-3/4" from either edge.

2. Glue the fuselage sides (A) to the vertical stabilizer (B). Take care

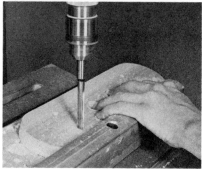

Drill holes for the wing struts (F) at a 15° angle.

LIST OF MATERIALS

(finished dimensions in inches)

A	Fuselage sides (2)	3/4 × 3-1/2 × 12
B	Vertical stabilizer	3/4 × 7 × 13-1/2
C	Horizontal stabilizers (2)	3/4 × 4-1/8 × 4-1/2
D	Top wing	3/4 × 4 × 14
E	Bottom wing	3/4 × 3-1/2 × 14
F	Wing struts (4)	3/8 dia. × 6-1/2
G	Cowling	3-1/2 dia. × 3/4
H	Propeller	1/2 × 1-3/8 × 6
J	Pivot	3/8 dia. × 2-1/2
K	Keeper	1 dia. × 1/2
L	Landing struts (2)	1 dia. × 2-1/2
M	Axle	3/8 dia. × 4-3/4
N	Wheels (2)	1-3/4 dia. × 3/4

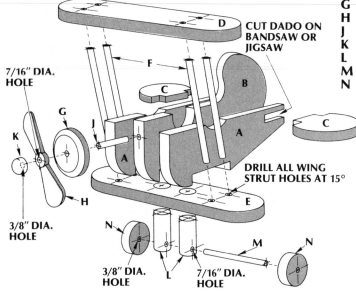

7/16" DIA. HOLE

CUT DADO ON BANDSAW OR JIGSAW

DRILL ALL WING STRUT HOLES AT 15°

3/8" DIA. HOLE

3/8" DIA. HOLE

7/16" DIA. HOLE

that the dadoes for the bottom wing line up exactly. Refer to pattern for position.

3. Glue the horizontal stabilizers (C) in the dadoes toward the rear of the fuselage sides (A).

4. Glue the landing struts (L) in the 1″ holes in the bottom wing (E), taking care the axle holes line up. Glue the wing struts (F) in the 3/8″ holes in the top wing (D); then, glue the other end of the struts in the 3/8″ holes in the bottom wing (E). When all is glued in place, the wing surfaces should be parallel and the wing's struts should stick out 1/8″ above and below the wings. Sand the struts flush with the wing surfaces.

5. Glue the wing assembly to the fuselage/stabilizer assembly, slipping the bottom wing (E) into the dado at the bottom of the fuselage. Reinforce the glue joint with dowels or screws.

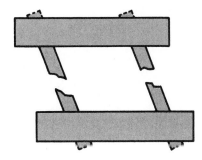

The wing surfaces should be parallel and the struts should protrude above and below just enough so that you can sand them down flush with the wings.

6. Glue the cowling (G) onto the front of the fuselage. If you wish, you can round the leading edge of the cowling with a rasp or sandpaper. Drill a 3/8″ hole through the center of the cowling, at least 3/4″ into the fuselage. Glue the pivot (J) in this hole.

7. Place the propeller (H) on the pivot (J). You can put a realistic pitch in the blades of the propeller with a rasp or sander. With the propeller in place, glue the keeper (K) on the pivot (J), leaving enough room for the propeller to turn freely.

8. Insert the axle (M) into the holes in the landing struts (L), and glue on the wheels (N).

Caution the aspiring pilot to whom you give this airplane that this is not a free-flying model. Flight plans should include a great deal of ground support.

ONE SQUARE = 1/2″

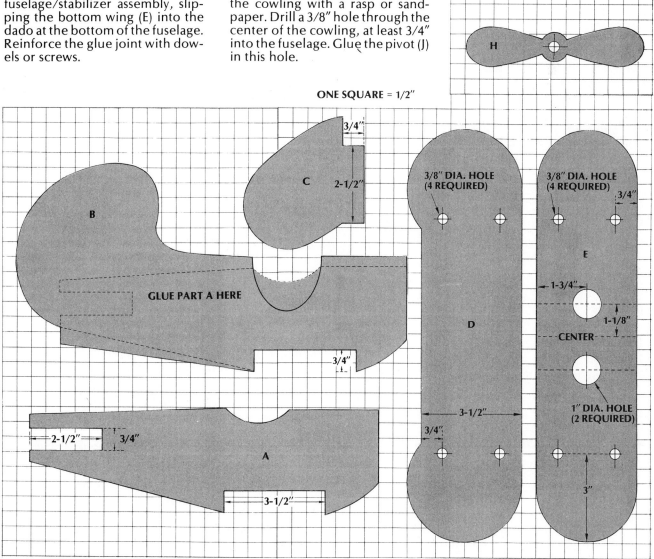

PECKING CHICKENS

From *HANDS ON* July/Aug 81

Old-fashioned toys, particularly animated ones, delight children of all ages and they are very popular at crafts fairs. You'll find yourself playing with these pecking chickens too. Swing the toy in a horizontal rotary motion and the four chickens peck, in order, at seeds in the center of the paddle.

Cut the paddle (A) out with a bandsaw or jigsaw, then round the edges. Drill all the holes in the paddle, countersinking the 1/8" diameter holes both on the top and bottom of the paddle to keep the string from snagging or wearing thin on the edges.

In the end grain of 3/4" thick stock, cut a 1/4" wide by 5/16" deep kerf with dado blades. This kerf forms the hinge in the body of the chickens (B) for the heads (C) to pivot. Lay out and cut the chicken bodies in a way that the kerf is at an angle to cause the heads of the chickens to tilt forward slightly. Then, drill a dowel hole in the bottom of each chicken body.

From 1/4" thick stock, cut out the chicken heads (C). Drill holes in the lower neck for the hinge and the string. Attach the strings and hinge each head to the bodies (B) with finishing nails, allowing enough room for the string to slide. Mount the chickens to the paddle (A) with dowels (D).

Feed the string through the holes in the paddle and fasten the strings to a bead, using a wedge to hold the strings tight. Make sure all four strings are the same length to pull equally. Tie a weight to the bead.

Finally, glue seeds in the center of the paddle close enough for the chickens to peck at, but not actually hit.

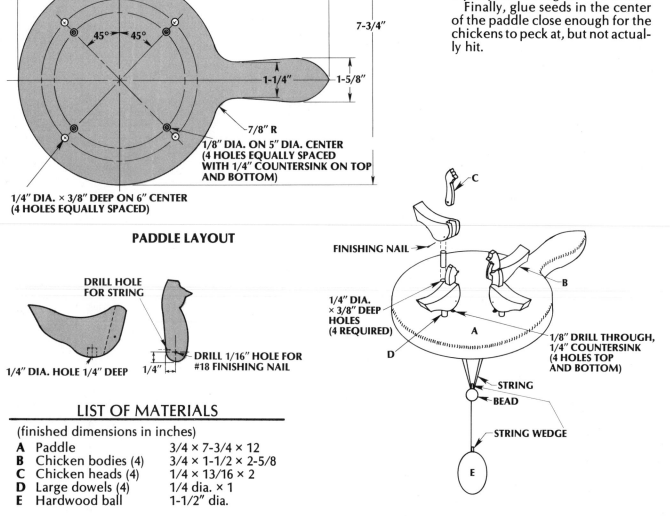

PADDLE LAYOUT

12"

45° 45°

7-3/4"

1-1/4"

1-5/8"

7/8" R

1/8" DIA. ON 5" DIA. CENTER (4 HOLES EQUALLY SPACED WITH 1/4" COUNTERSINK ON TOP AND BOTTOM)

1/4" DIA. × 3/8" DEEP ON 6" CENTER (4 HOLES EQUALLY SPACED)

DRILL HOLE FOR STRING

1/4" DIA. HOLE 1/4" DEEP

1/4"

DRILL 1/16" HOLE FOR #18 FINISHING NAIL

C

FINISHING NAIL

1/4" DIA. × 3/8" DEEP HOLES (4 REQUIRED)

B

A

D

1/8" DRILL THROUGH, 1/4" COUNTERSINK (4 HOLES TOP AND BOTTOM)

STRING

BEAD

STRING WEDGE

E

LIST OF MATERIALS

(finished dimensions in inches)

A	Paddle	3/4 × 7-3/4 × 12
B	Chicken bodies (4)	3/4 × 1-1/2 × 2-5/8
C	Chicken heads (4)	1/4 × 13/16 × 2
D	Large dowels (4)	1/4 dia. × 1
E	Hardwood ball	1-1/2" dia.

The Climbing Bear is a favorite of children and adults and it's an easy project to mass produce. Here's how.

Begin by making a hardboard template of the bear design and a support fixture to aid in drilling the bear's paws.

Cut blanks and bars to size. Stack four blanks, tape together, and trace the bear pattern on the top. Cut out the design with a bandsaw, then sand away the millmarks with a strip sander while the bears are still stacked up.

Now for the drilling: Tilt the table to 55° and, with the bears square against the support fixture, drill 3/16" holes through the paws. Reset the table to 90° and drill 3/16" holes in the bars.

Add face decoration to one or both sides of the bears. Cut jute or sash cord into pieces 50" and 8" long. To assemble, thread the 50" cords through the bears, bars, and beads, and knot the ends. Use the 8" cords as center supports, passing them through the bars and beads, and making loops.

To make the bear climb, hang the support loop from a nail or hook. First pull one cord, then the other, and the bear will shimmy up to the bar. Release both the cords and the bear will slide back down.

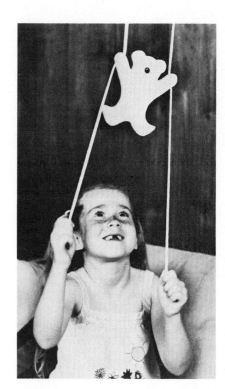

SASH CORD

LIST OF MATERIALS

(finished dimensions in inches)

A	Body	3/4 × 5 × 5-3/4
B	Bar	1/2 × 3/4 × 6-3/4
C	Beads (3)	1/2 dia.
D	Cord	5/32 dia. × 8

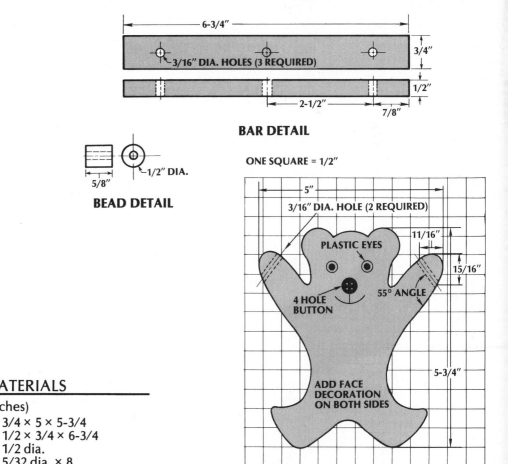

6-3/4"

3/16" DIA. HOLES (3 REQUIRED)

3/4"

2-1/2"

7/8"

1/2"

BAR DETAIL

5/8"

1/2" DIA.

BEAD DETAIL

ONE SQUARE = 1/2"

5"

3/16" DIA. HOLE (2 REQUIRED)

PLASTIC EYES

11/16"

15/16"

4 HOLE BUTTON

55° ANGLE

5-3/4"

ADD FACE DECORATION ON BOTH SIDES

DOLL CRADLE

From *HANDS ON* Nov/Dec 79

The wood requirements for this project are minimal. The entire cradle can be made out of one 8' piece of 1 × 12 lumber. The curves in the rockers, headboard, footboard, and sides can be easily cut with a jigsaw, sabre saw, bandsaw, or coping saw. Simple construction techniques are followed throughout, but the results are wonderful. This project will win the heart of any little girl.

1. Cut all pieces using the patterns provided and the List of Materials. When cutting the rockers (A), take care that the grain of the wood runs horizontally for maximum strength. The bottom edge of the sideboards (C) should be cut on a 10° angle so they sit flat against the base. To cut the decoration at the top of the headboard (E), drill a 1" hole center 1-1/8" from the top edge. Then, open up the hole with your bandsaw or jigsaw.

Opening up a hole with a bandsaw to make the decoration at the top of the headboard (E).

2. Glue the sideboards (C) to the footboard (D) and headboard (E). Reinforce the glue joints with dowels or screws.
3. Shape or rout a decorative edge on the base (B). Use a quarter-round bead, or feel free to use any design you want.
4. Glue the rockers (A) to the base (B). The rockers should be positioned 2" from the head and foot of the base. Reinforce the glue joints.
5. Glue the side/foot/headboard assembly to the base/rocker assembly, centering the side, foot, and headboards on the base. Reinforce with screws.

Every doll needs a place to rest its head—ask any little girl. The Doll Cradle has been popular with children since the invention of dolls. And this Shaker-design cradle makes a cozy place to bed down.

LIST OF MATERIALS

(finished dimensions in inches)

A	Rockers (2)	3/4 × 4 × 18
B	Base	3/4 × 11 × 20
C	Sideboards (2)	3/4 × 8 × 19
D	Footboard	3/4 × 5-3/8 × 10-1/4
E	Headboard	3/4 × 10-1/4 × 11-1/4

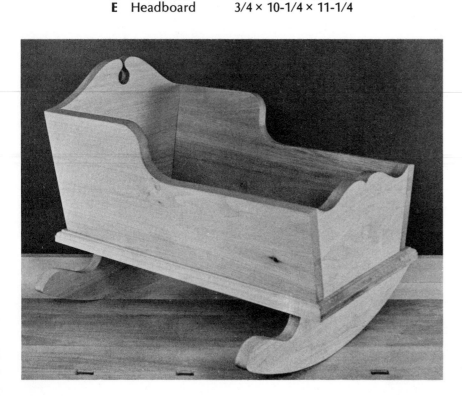

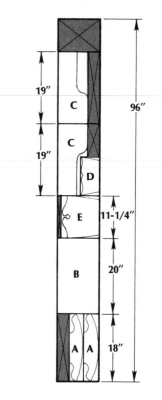

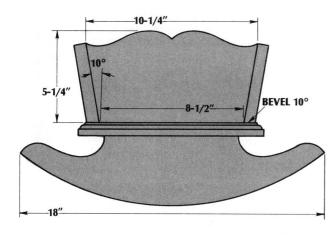

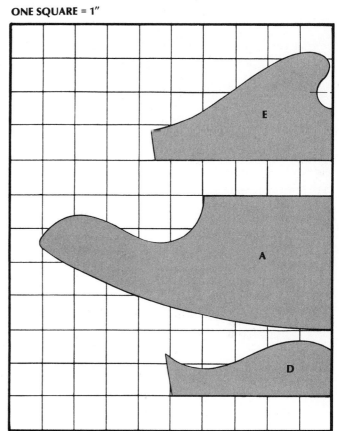

ONE SQUARE = 1"

E

A

D

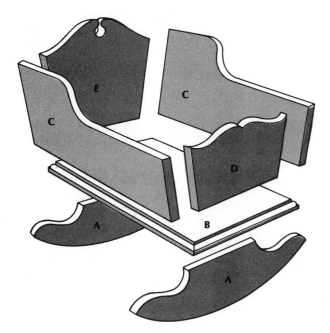

E

C

C

D

A

B

A

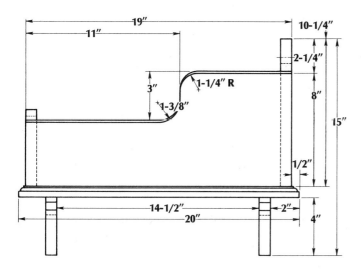

19"

11"

10-1/4"

2-1/4"

3"

1-1/4" R

1-3/8"

8"

15"

1/2"

14-1/2"

20"

2"

4"

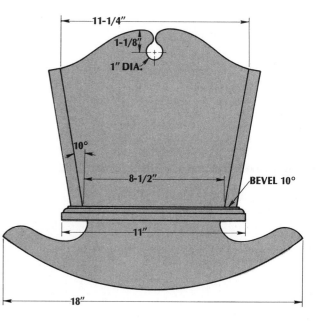

11-1/4"

1-1/8"

1" DIA.

10°

8-1/2"

BEVEL 10°

11"

18"

10-1/4"

10°

5-1/4"

8-1/2"

BEVEL 10°

18"

ROCKING PLANE

From *HANDS ON* Sept/Oct 82

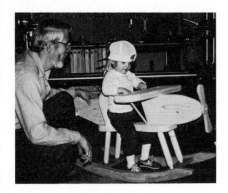

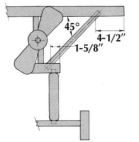

Any junior pilot will enjoy riding in this airplane. Playtime will become a new adventure. Build this rocking toy for a child and you'll feel deep satisfaction.

1. Cut all pieces to size, according to the List of Materials; then, lay out the seat (A), nose (B), wing (C), seat back (D), tail (E), stabilizer (F), rockers (G), and propeller (H). Groove the seat back for the tail, then cut the hand slots in the wing. Next, cut all contours on the bandsaw or jigsaw.

2. Turn the four legs (J) and the hub (K) on the lathe out of 2 × 2 stock. When you turn the 3/4" diameter tenons on the ends of the legs and the hub, use your calipers to check the diameters.

3. Drill the 3/4" holes required in the seat (A) by using the drill press mode with the worktable tilted

15°. Then drill 3/4" holes at 90° in the stretchers (L) for the legs (J). Also drill the 3/4" holes for the propeller hub (K) and for the struts (M). Holes for the struts are drilled at 45°. Dry-assemble the seat, legs, and stretchers to locate the position of the rockers (G). Drill 3/8" dowel holes for joining the stretchers to the rockers. Finally drill 1/2" dowel holes to join all remaining parts. Use brad point bits for clean and accurate holes.

4. Bevel the propeller (H) on the belt sander to add pitch to the blade.

5. Round off all exposed edges with the shaper, router, or a wood rasp and sand the project. Sharp corners and edges pose a danger for small children.

6. Assemble all parts with woodworker's glue, then apply a non-toxic finish.

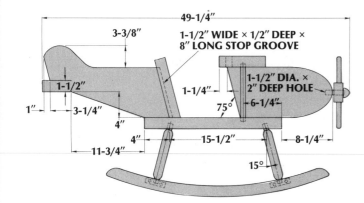

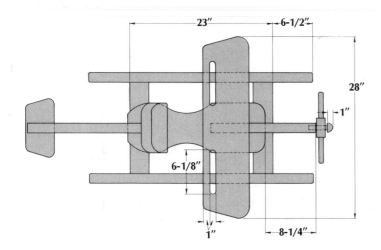

LIST OF MATERIALS

(finished dimensions in inches)

A	Seat	1-1/2 × 7-1/4 × 22
B	Nose	1-1/2 × 7-1/4 × 17
C	Wing	1-1/2 × 7-1/4 × 28
D	Seat back	1-1/2 × 7-1/4 × 9-1/2
E	Tail	1-1/2 × 11 × 16
F	Stabilizer	1-1/2 × 4-1/2 × 9
G	Rockers (2)	1-1/2 × 5 × 36
H	Propeller	1-1/2 × 3-1/2 × 10
J	Legs (4)	1-1/2 dia. × 10
K	Hub	1-1/2 dia. × 4-1/2
L	Stretchers (2)	3/4 × 3 × 14
M	Struts (2)	3/4 dia. × 12
	Dowels (13)	1/2 dia. × 3
	Dowels (8)	3/8 dia. × 1-1/2

Children often play house, mimicking their mother and father. With their own kitchen, kids can pretend to bake and cook, without burning a finger or distracting the real cook. This toy kitchen is easily constructed from two sheets of 1/2" particleboard and a few pieces of hardware.

1. Cut all pieces to size by following the cutout diagrams provided and the List of Materials. You'll need a helper to cut the 4 × 8 sheets of particleboard safely. Cut out the sink opening in the countertop (D).

2. Assemble with nails and glue the right side of the refrigerator (B) to the bottom (A). Attach shelves (G, H), sides (B), top (E), and stove sides (C) and shelves (J), going from the right side to the left.

3. Attach the back (F) to this assembly. Bolt the stove door (N) to the kickboard (K) and attach this assembly. Then, attach the refrigerator kickboard (L).

4. Mount the refrigerator doors (P, Q) with strap hinges. First, screw the hinges to the inside of the doors; then, attach them to the side of the refrigerator. If you want the hinges mounted flush, you'll need to cut a notch in the side to recess the hinge.

5. Paint the kitchen the color of your choice, and use self-adhering vinyl shelf covering behind the stove for a finished effect. Use black paint to create spiral burners.

6. Make and attach accessories such as the faucets, knobs, and sink. The sink can be a plastic pan or tray. Make faucets as in the plans, or use discarded faucets for enhanced playability.

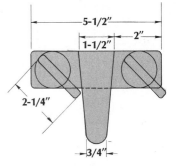

FAUCET DETAIL

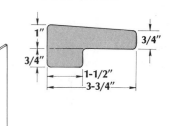

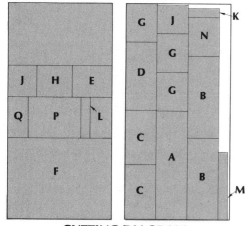

CUTTING DIAGRAM

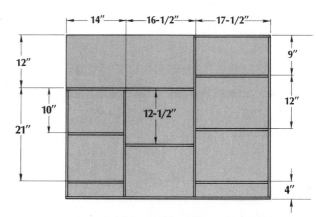

NOTE: DOORS (N, P, Q) NOT SHOWN.

LIST OF MATERIALS

(finished dimensions in inches)

A	Bottom	1/2 × 14 × 48
B	Refrigerator sides (2)	1/2 × 14 × 36
C	Stove sides (2)	1/2 × 14 × 24
D	Countertop	1/2 × 14 × 30
E	Refrigerator top	1/2 × 14 × 18
F	Back	1/2 × 37 × 48
G	Refrigerator shelves (3)	1/2 × 14 × 17
H	Shelf	1/2 × 14 × 16
J	Stove shelves (2)	1/2 × 13 × 14
K	Stove kickboard	1/2 × 4 × 14
L	Refrigerator kickboard	1/2 × 4 × 18
M	Sink front	1/2 × 4 × 30
N	Stove door	1/2 × 14 × 17
P	Refrigerator door	1/2 × 18 × 24
Q	Freezer door	1/2 × 9 × 18

NOTE: DOORS (N, P, Q) AND FACING STRIPS (K, L, M) NOT SHOWN.

SPACE SHUTTLE

From *HANDS ON* Nov/Dec 79

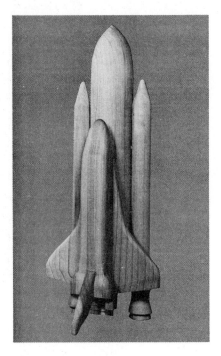

In 1981, the world's first true spaceship—the Space Shuttle—lifted off on its maiden voyage. It is planned that shuttles will ferry dozens of astronauts between earth and outer space, making spaceflight as common to our children as air travel is to us. Here is a toy Space Shuttle for those young people who will one day become part of space travel.

1. Cut all pieces to the proper size and shape. Turn the rockets (E), external fuel tank (F), and the booster rockets (G) on a lathe.

2. Round the leading edge and taper the trailing edge of the vertical stabilizer (A) and the wings (C), using a rasp or sander. Areas that join to other pieces should not be rounded or tapered. Round and taper only the areas that are shaded on the patterns. Also, round the rocket pods (D).

LIST OF MATERIALS

(finished dimensions in inches)

A	Vertical stabilizer	3/4 × 6 × 15-7/8
B	Fuselage sides (2)	3/4 × 3 × 14-1/8
C	Wings	3/4 × 10 × 10-1/2
D	Rocket pods (2)	3/4 × 1-1/2 × 2-5/8
E	Rockets (3)	1-1/4 dia. × 1-1/4
F	External fuel tank	3-1/2 dia. × 19-1/2
G	Booster rockets (2)	2 dia. × 19
H	Pegs (9)	3/8 dia. × 1

Tapering the vertical stabilizer (A) with a belt sander.

3. Glue the fuselage sides (B) to either side of the vertical stabilizer (A), taking care that the dadoes for the wings line up. Round the nose of the fuselage with a rasp or sander. Glue the wings (C) in place. Glue the rocket pods (D) to either side of the fuselage.

Round the rocket pods (D) and the nose of the Shuttle as shown.

4. Drill a 3/8" hole 1/2" deep in the narrow end of the three rockets (E). Drill three more 3/8" holes 1/2" deep in the rear of the shuttle assembly. Glue pegs (H) in the 3/8" holes in the rockets (E), then glue the other end of the pegs in the holes in the rear of the shuttle assembly. When mounted, rockets should clear the vertical stabilizer (A) and the bottom edge of the shuttle by at least 1/4".

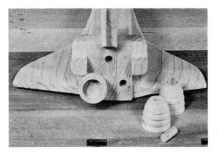

The rockets (E) are pegged to the back of the Shuttle.

5. Drill two 3/8" holes 1/2" deep, 4" and 9" from the bottom (round end) of the external fuel tank (F). Rotate the tank 90° and drill two more holes the same distance from the bottom. Rotate the tank 90° again and drill two more. Drill two 3/8" holes 1/2" deep in each of the booster rockets (G), 8" and 13" from the bottom. Glue pegs (H) in the holes in the booster rockets;

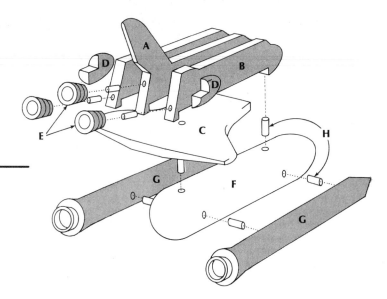

then, sand the protruding ends of these pegs until they fit snugly, but not too snugly, in the holes in the external fuel tank (F). Mount (but *don't* glue) the two booster rockets (G) on opposite sides of the external fuel tank (F), fitting the pegs in the holes.

6. Using a carpenter's square, stand the shuttle assembly on its vertical stabilizer (A), belly perpendicular to the floor. Mark the belly 8" and 13" up from the floor. Drill two 3/8" holes 1/2" deep at these marks, centered in the belly. Glue two pegs (H) in the two remaining holes

in the external fuel tank (F). These pegs should be 90° away from both the booster rockets. Sand the protruding ends of the pegs so they fit snugly into the holes of the belly of the shuttle assembly. Mount (but *don't* glue) the shuttle to the external fuel tank.

The Shuttle, the external fuel tank, and the booster rockets should all peg together and pop apart easily.

Now comes a moment of truth. In the launch position, the Space Shuttle should rest on the booster rockets (G) and vertical stabilizer (A), pointing straight at the stars. A few moments after liftoff (from your workbench), the booster rockets should separate easily and float back to earth while the shuttle and its external fuel tank continue upward. Upon reaching orbit (an arm's length above your head), the tank disengages. The Space Shuttle then completes its mission and glides back to your workbench for reassembly—and another mission.

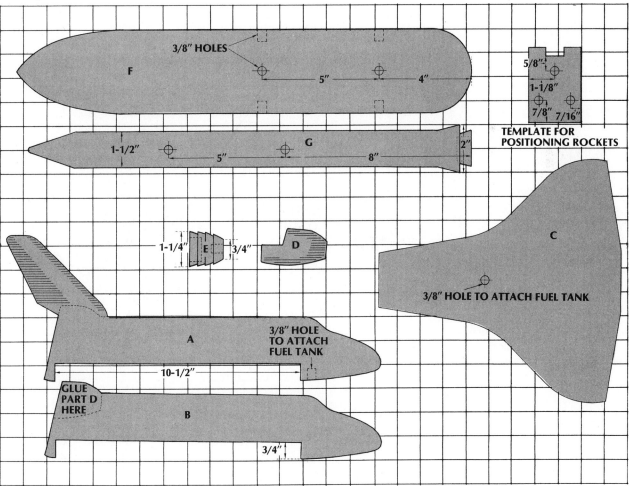

From *HANDS ON* Nov/Dec 79

The first toy train appeared in the 1820s—only a few years after the first train. As railroads grew and locomotive designs developed and diversified, so did toy trains. But the favorite remains this classic 4-4-0 from the Golden Age of Steam.

THE LOCOMOTIVE

1. Cut all pieces to the proper size and shape, using the patterns provided and the List of Materials. Drill 7/16" axle holes in wheel mounts (D, E) and a 7/16" hole in engine coupler (F). Refer to patterns for position of these holes.

Drill 3/8" holes in the center of wheels (L, M). Turn pistons (N), boiler (O), smokestack (P), and pressure dome (Q) on lathe.

2. Glue up platform sections (A, B, C). Refer to pattern for position. Cut cowcatcher with a compound miter cut—set the table at 30° and the miter gauge at 60°.

Cut the cowcatcher when the upper, mid, and lower platforms (A, B, C) have been glued up. The table is tilted at 30°; the miter gauge at 60°. **Note: Guard removed for clarity only.**

3. Glue the upper cab sides (I) to lower cab sides (J). Refer to pattern and exploded view for position—lower cab sides should protrude 3/4" below upper cab sides. Glue cab sides to firewall (H). Glue on cab roof (K). Roof should be pitched at 15°. Reinforce glue joints with dowels or screws.

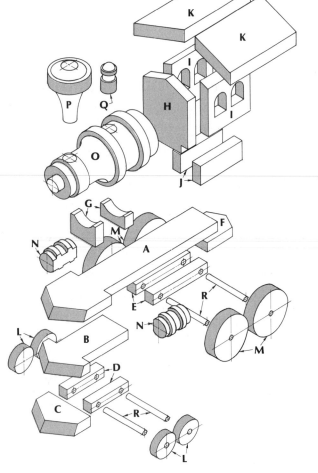

LIST OF MATERIALS

(finished dimensions in inches)

The Locomotive

A	Upper platform	3/4 × 3-3/4 × 15-1/2
B	Mid platform	3/4 × 3-3/4 × 7
C	Lower platform	3/4 × 3-3/4 × 2-3/4
D	Truck wheel mounts (2)	3/4 × 3/4 × 3-1/2
E	Drive wheel mounts (2)	3/4 × 3/4 × 5
F	Engine coupler	3/4 × 2-1/4 × 3
G	Boiler mounts (2)	3/4 × 2 × 2-1/4
H	Firewall	3/4 × 3-3/4 × 5
I	Upper cab sides (2)	3/4 × 3-7/8 × 4
J	Lower cab sides (2)	3/4 × 1-1/2 × 4
K	Cab roof (2)	3/4 × 2-3/8 × 6-1/4
L	Truck wheels (4)	1-3/4 dia. × 3/4
M	Drive wheels (4)	3-1/4 dia. × 3/4
N	Pistons (2)	1-3/8 dia. × 2-1/8
O	Boiler	3-3/4 dia. × 7-1/2
P	Smokestack	2-3/4 dia. × 4-1/4
Q	Pressure dome	1 dia. × 2
R	Axles	3/8 dia. × 3-7/8

4. Glue boiler (O) to boiler mounts (G). Reinforce glue joints. Drill 1" holes for smokestack (P) and pressure dome (Q). Refer to pattern for position.

5. Temporarily assemble wheels to mounts. Position wheel assemblies under the platform; the boiler and cab assemblies on top of the platform. Back of the drive wheels (M) should be flush with the back of the cab; the truck wheels (L) must not rub on the cowcatcher. When you have the assemblies properly lined up, mark for position and disassemble.

6. Glue on boiler and cab assemblies. Reinforce.

7. Glue truck wheel mounts (D), drive wheel mounts (E), and engine coupler (F) to platform. Take care that all axle holes line up. Refer to pattern for position of coupler. Reinforce.

8. Insert axles (R) in mounts and glue on wheels.

The underside of the engine shows the reinforcing screws before they are covered with dowels.

9. Sand a flat spot 3/4" wide on the pistons (N) and glue in position over rear truck wheels (L). Reinforce.

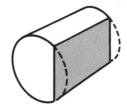

10. Glue smokestack (P) and pressure dome (Q) in holes on top of boiler (O).

THE COAL CAR

1. Cut all pieces to the proper size and shape, using patterns provided and the List of Materials. Drill 7/16" axle holes in the drive wheel mounts (E), a 7/16" hole in the car coupler (U), and 3/8" holes in the coal car platform (V) and the center of the truck wheels (L). Refer to pattern for position of holes.

2. Glue coal car sides (W) to coal car back (X). Glue coal car assembly to coal car platform (V). Reinforce.

3. Glue drive wheel mounts (E) to coal car truck mount (T), taking care that axle holes line up. Glue car coupler (U) to coal car assembly. Refer to pattern for position. Reinforce.

4. Temporarily assemble wheels to mount. Place coal car assembly on truck assembly and mark for position. Wheels must not rub on car coupler. Disassemble.

5. Glue truck assembly to coal car assembly. Reinforce. Insert axles (R) in mounts and glue on truck wheels (L). Glue coupler pin (S) in hole in coal car platform (V). Pin should extend 3/4" below platform.

THE BASIC CAR

Many different cars can be made to follow the locomotive and coal car, all mounted on a basic car assembly.

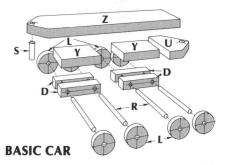

The basic car and a bottom view of a basic truck assembly.

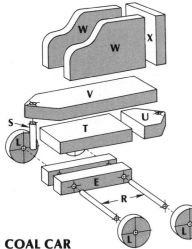

COAL CAR

BASIC CAR

LIST OF MATERIALS

(finished dimensions in inches)

The Coal Car

E	Drive wheel mounts (2)	3/4 × 3/4 × 5
L	Truck wheels (4)	1-3/4 dia. × 3/4
R	Axles (2)	3/8 dia. × 3-7/8
S	Coupler pin	3/8 dia. × 1-1/2
T	Coal car truck mount	3/4 × 2-1/4 × 5
U	Car coupler	3/4 × 3-3/4 × 3
V	Coal car platform	3/4 × 3-3/4 × 8
W	Coal car sides (2)	3/4 × 3 × 5
X	Coal car back	3/4 × 3-3/4 × 3

LIST OF MATERIALS

(finished dimensions in inches)

The Basic Car

D	Truck wheel mounts (4)	3/4 × 3/4 × 3-1/2
L	Truck wheels (8)	1-3/4 dia. × 3/4
R	Axles (4)	3/8 dia. × 3-7/8
S	Coupler pin	3/8 dia. × 1-1/2
U	Car coupler	3/4 × 3-3/4 × 3
Y	Truck mounts (2)	3/4 × 2-1/4 × 3-1/2
Z	Car platform	3/4 × 3-3/4 × 13-1/2

1. Cut all pieces to the proper size and shape. Drill 7/16″ axle holes in truck wheel mounts (D), a 7/16″ hole in the car coupler (U), and 3/8″ holes in the car platform (Z) and the center of the truck wheels (L). Refer to pattern for position of holes.
2. Glue special car assembly (log car, box car, etc.) to car platform (Z) *before* assembling basic car.
3. Glue truck wheel mounts (D) to truck mounts (Y), taking care that axle holes line up. Glue car coupler (U) to car platform (Z). Refer to pattern for position. Reinforce.
4. Temporarily assemble wheels to mounts. Place car assembly on top of truck assemblies and mark for position. Truck mounts (Y) should be approximately 2-1/4″ apart and wheels should not rub on coupler. Disassemble.
5. Glue truck assemblies in position and reinforce. Insert axles (R) in mounts and glue on wheels.

Glue coupler pin (S) in hole in car platform (Z). Pin should extend 3/4″ below platform.
Design and build as many cars for the train as your child can push along. Here are three suggestions:

THE FLAT CAR

1. Cut the basic car pieces and 10 extra axles. Drill ten 3/8″ holes in the car platform (Z). Holes should be spaced 2-3/16″ apart in two rows 3″ apart, 3/8″ in from either edge of the platform.
2. Glue axles (R) in these holes, protruding above the platform.
3. Assemble basic car.

THE BOX CAR

1. Cut basic car pieces and pieces listed for box car.
2. Glue box car sides (DD) to car front and back (CC). Reinforce. Glue box car side/front/back assemblies to car platform (Z), leaving a 3″ space between assemblies for doors. Reinforce.
3. Cut a 5/16″ × 5/16″ deep rabbet in the tops and bottoms of the box car doors (EE). Drill a 3/8″ hole midway up the doors, 3/8″ from one side, as shown:

BOX CAR DOOR DETAIL

LIST OF MATERIALS

(finished dimensions in inches)

The Flat Car

All materials listed for the basic car, plus:

R   Axles (10)   3/8 dia. × 3-7/8

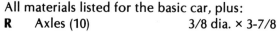

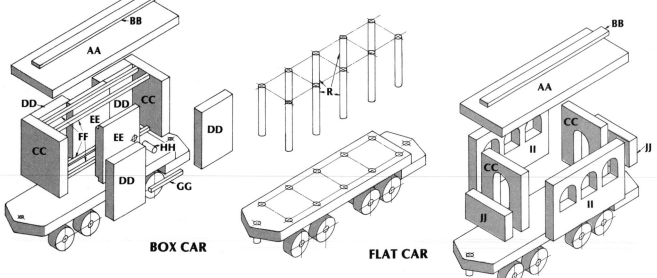

BOX CAR

FLAT CAR

PULLMAN

LIST OF MATERIALS

(finished dimensions in inches)

The Box Car

All materials listed for the basic car, plus:

AA	Car top	3/4 × 4 × 12
BB	Top rail	1/4 × 3/4 × 11-1/2
CC	Car front/back (2)	3/4 × 3-3/4 × 4-1/2
DD	Box car sides (4)	3/4 × 3 × 4-1/2
EE	Box car doors (2)	3/4 × 3-1/2 × 4-7/16
FF	Inside door slides (4)	1/4 × 1/4 × 9
GG	Outside door slides (2)	1/4 × 1/4 × 3
HH	Door pulls (2)	3/8 dia. × 1

LIST OF MATERIALS

(finished dimensions in inches)

The Pullman

All materials listed for the basic car, plus:

AA	Car top	3/4 × 4 × 12
BB	Top rail	1/4 × 3/4 × 11-1/2
CC	Car front/back (2)	3/4 × 3-3/4 × 4-1/2
II	Pullman sides (2)	3/4 × 4-1/2 × 6-3/4
JJ	Observation railings (2)	3/4 × 2 × 3-3/4

ONE SQUARE = 1"

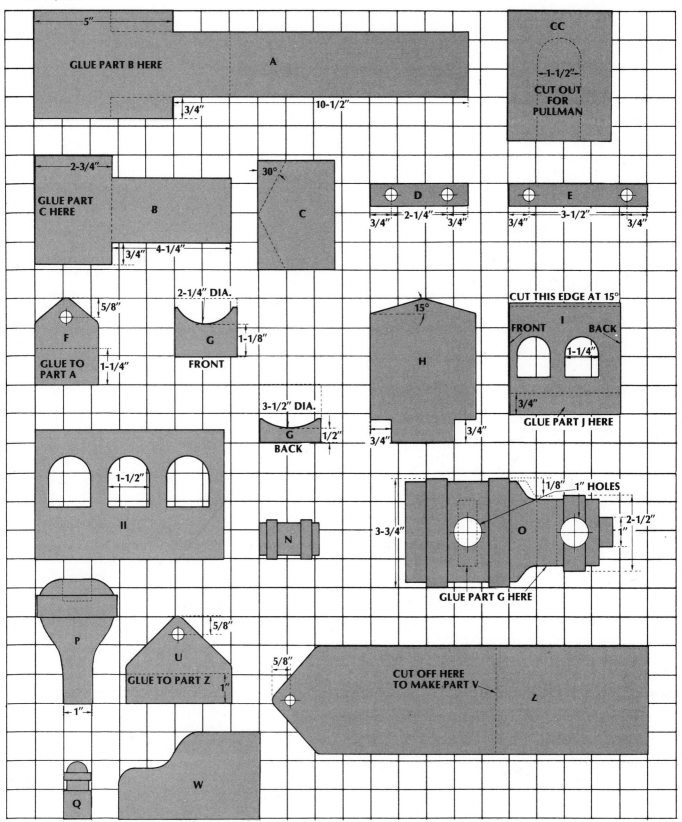

Glue door pulls (HH) in holes with end protruding from side *opposite* rabbets.

4. Glue two inside door slides (FF) to car platform (Z), 1/2" away from the box car sides (DD). Position doors in place with rabbets riding on the slides. Carefully position the two remaining inside door slides (FF) in the top rabbets, 1/2" away from the sides, and flush with the top of the box car assembly. Check to see that doors slide easily. Glue upper inside slides in place with a drop of glue at each end.

The rabbets in the box car doors (EE) ride on the inside door slides (FF).

5. Spread a liberal amount of glue on the top of the box car sides, front, back, and upper inside door slides, and glue the car top (AA) in place. Reinforce. Glue the top rail (BB) down the middle of the car top (AA). Glue the outside door slides (GG) to the car platform (Z), the inside edge flush with the inside edge of the box car sides (DD).

6. Assemble basic car.

THE PULLMAN

1. Cut the basic car pieces and pieces listed for the Pullman using the patterns provided.

The windows in the upper cab sides (I) of the Locomotive and the Pullman sides (II) can be cut with a jigsaw or coping saw, using an internal piercing cut.

2. Glue car front and back (CC) to Pullman sides (II). Glue car top (AA) to Pullman assembly. Top should stick out 1-7/8" front and back. Reinforce. Glue top rail (BB) down the middle of the car top (AA).

3. Temporarily position Pullman assembly and observation railings (JJ) on car platform (Z). Railings should be 1-1/8" away from the front and back. Mark for position; then, glue in place and reinforce.

4. Assemble basic car.

If you build a long train, a locomotive and several cars, you may find it timesaving to cut the pieces (wheels, mounts, platforms, etc.) all at once. Look over the List of Materials, add up the number and type of pieces you need, and set up for mass production.

One more tip: When you finish assembling your train, get down on the floor, hook the cars together, and play with it to your heart's content. Once you give this to a child you'll never have the chance again—unless you build one of your own.

There must be a few things more exciting to a child than a fire engine, but we can't think of any. We chose to build the most exciting of fire engines: the hook and ladder.

1. Cut all pieces to size and shape, except ladder rails, according to the List of Materials.

A quick, easy way to make perfectly round wheels is with a hole saw and then sanding them smooth on a lathe or drill press. Then, if you want, put a decorative groove in the side of each wheel on a lathe with a skew chisel.

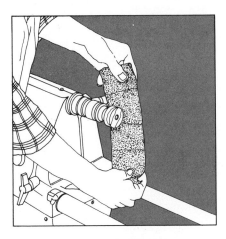

Sand wheels smooth on a lathe.

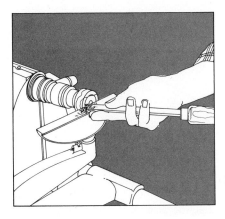

Cut decorative groove in side of wheel on a lathe.

2. Drill holes as shown on patterns, except the truck bodies and ladders. Also, drill 3/8" holes in the center of the wheels (D), a 1/4" hole through the center of the reel crank (W), and a second 1/4" hole in the reel crank, 3/8" in from the edge.

3. Glue the truck bodies (A) and drill holes as shown on patterns.

4. Insert the two axles (E) in the truck body axle holes and glue on wheels (D). Position the fenders so that the wheels don't rub in the wells and glue in place. If you wish, round the fenders with a rasp or sander. Also, round the back corners of the truck assembly as shown in the truck body exploded view. Reinforce the fender glue joints with dowels or screws.

Round fenders with a belt sander.

5. Drill two 1/2" holes in the front of the truck assembly, with the centers 3/4" in from the outside edge of the fenders and 1-3/8" up from the bottom edge. Insert headlights (F) and glue in place.

6. Sand a 3/4" flat spot on the water tank (C) and glue in place in back of truck seat. Reinforce the glue joint with a dowel pin.

7. Glue the six platform supports (J) into the 3/8" holes in the lower platform (G). Then, glue the supports in the corresponding holes in the upper platform (H). The rounded ends of the platforms should face the same direction and be 1-1/2" apart.

8. The telescoping ladder slides together by means of a 5/32" groove that runs the length of the telescoping ladder rails (Q). It's easiest to cut this groove with an ordinary saw blade *before* you rip the ladder rail from the wood stock. The groove should be 5/32" deep and 1/8" from the edge of the rails.

Drill holes on the pivoting and sliding ladders. Skip a hole at one end of the two pivoting ladder rails (Q) that will attach to the pivot block (L).

9. Assemble pivoting ladder and attach to pivot block (L). Assemble sliding ladder and slide into pivoting ladder.

(continues on next page)

10. Attach a peg (M) in groove to pivoting ladder as a stop to keep the sliding ladder from scraping against the pivot block (L). Rip other ladder rails to size and drill rung holes; then, assemble.

11. Glue a wheel (D) to the lower side of the upper platform (H), lining up the hole in the wheel with the forward hole in the platform. Drill a 1/4" hole 1/4" from the end of the coupler (K). Glue a peg (M) in this hole, so that 3/16" of the peg protrudes on each side. Pass the coupler through the 7/16" hole in the pivot block (L) and insert the forward hole in the upper platform (H). When glued in place, coupler should extend 3/4" below the platform and wheel, and still allow the pivot block and telescoping ladder assembly to turn freely. The peg in the ladder will serve as a keeper for the ladder assembly.

12. Glue the ladder hooks (S) in the 3/8" × 1/2" deep holes in the edge of the upper platform (H). Glue pegs (M) into the holes, with 3/8" of the pegs protruding above the hooks. Hang assembled ladders on hooks.

13. Assemble the hose reel (T), reel supports (U), reel pivot (V), and reel crank (W) as shown in ex-

LIST OF MATERIALS

(finished dimensions in inches)

A	Truck bodies (3)	3/4 × 3 × 9-3/4
B	Fenders (2)	3/4 × 2-1/4 × 5-1/4
C	Water tank	1-1/4 dia. × 2-1/4
D	Wheels (9)	1-3/4 dia. × 3/4
E	Axles (4)	3/8 dia. × 3-7/8
F	Headlights (2)	1/2 dia. × 3/4
G	Lower platform	3/4 × 3-3/4 × 15-1/2
H	Upper platform	3/4 × 2-1/4 × 15-1/2
J	Platform supports (6)	3/8 dia. × 3
K	Coupler	3/8 dia. × 3-1/2
L	Pivot block	3/4 × 3/4 × 1
M	Pegs (9)	1/4 dia. × 3/4
N	Ladder rails (4)	1/4 × 3/4 × 12
P	Ladder rungs (33)	1/4 dia. × 1-3/4
Q	Telescoping ladder rails (4)	1/4 × 3/4 × 13
R	Telescoping ladder rungs (12)	1/4 dia. × 1-1/2
S	Ladder hooks (4)	3/8 dia. × 1-1/2
T	Hose reel	1-1/2 dia. × 2-1/8
U	Reel supports (2)	3/4 × 1-1/2 × 2
V	Reel pivot	1/4 dia. × 4-1/8
W	Reel crank	1-1/2 dia. × 3/8
X	Hose	1/4 dia. × 48 nylon rope
Y	Nozzle	3/8 dia. × 1

ploded view. Glue hose assembly on lower platform (G).

14. Pass axles (E) through 7/16" axle holes in lower platform (G) and glue on wheels (D).

15. Hook the coupler (K) into the hole in the back of the truck body, and you have a hook and ladder capable of rescuing people from burning buildings almost 2' high.

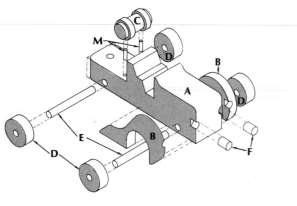

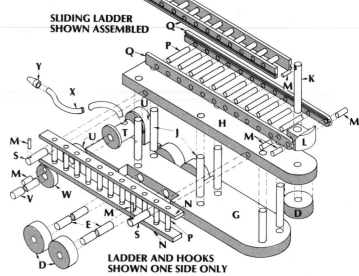

SLIDING LADDER SHOWN ASSEMBLED

LADDER AND HOOKS SHOWN ONE SIDE ONLY

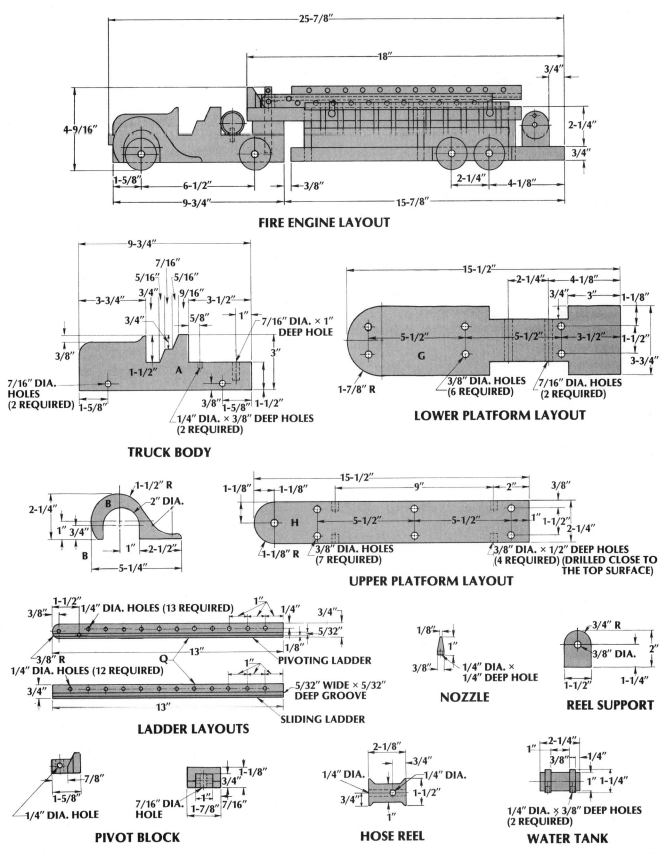

FIRE ENGINE LAYOUT

25-7/8"
18"
3/4"
4-9/16"
2-1/4"
3/4"
1-5/8"
6-1/2"
3/8"
2-1/4"
4-1/8"
9-3/4"
15-7/8"

TRUCK BODY

9-3/4"
7/16"
5/16"
5/16"
3/4"
9/16"
3-1/2"
3/4"
5/8"
1"
7/16" DIA. × 1"
DEEP HOLE
3/8"
3"
1-1/2" A
7/16" DIA.
HOLES
(2 REQUIRED)
1-5/8"
3/8"
1-5/8"
1-1/2"
1/4" DIA. × 3/8" DEEP HOLES
(2 REQUIRED)

LOWER PLATFORM LAYOUT

15-1/2"
2-1/4"
4-1/8"
3/4"
3"
1-1/8"
5-1/2"
5-1/2"
3-1/2"
1-1/2"
G
1-1/2"
3-3/4"
1-7/8" R
3/8" DIA. HOLES
(6 REQUIRED)
7/16" DIA. HOLES
(2 REQUIRED)

UPPER PLATFORM LAYOUT

15-1/2"
9"
2"
3/8"
1-1/8"
1-1/8"
5-1/2"
5-1/2"
1"
1-1/2"
H
2-1/4"
1-1/8" R
3/8" DIA. HOLES
(7 REQUIRED)
3/8" DIA. × 1/2" DEEP HOLES
(4 REQUIRED) (DRILLED CLOSE TO
THE TOP SURFACE)

1-1/2" R
2" DIA.
2-1/4"
B
1"
3/4"
1"
2-1/2"
B
5-1/4"

LADDER LAYOUTS

1-1/2"
1/4" DIA. HOLES (13 REQUIRED)
1"
1/4"
3/4"
3/8"
5/32"
3/8" R
1/8"
13"
Q
PIVOTING LADDER
1/4" DIA. HOLES (12 REQUIRED)
1"
3/4"
5/32" WIDE × 5/32"
DEEP GROOVE
13"
SLIDING LADDER

NOZZLE

1/8"
1"
3/8"
1/4" DIA. ×
1/4" DEEP HOLE

REEL SUPPORT

3/4" R
3/8" DIA.
2"
1-1/2"
1-1/4"

PIVOT BLOCK

7/8"
1-5/8"
1/4" DIA. HOLE
1-1/8"
3/4"
1"
7/16"
7/16" DIA.
HOLE
1-7/8"

HOSE REEL

2-1/8"
3/4"
1/4" DIA.
1/4" DIA.
3/4"
1-1/2"
1"

WATER TANK

2-1/4"
1"
3/8"
1/4"
1"
1-1/4"
1/4" DIA. × 3/8" DEEP HOLES
(2 REQUIRED)

TOY TOP

From *HANDS ON* Sept/Oct 81

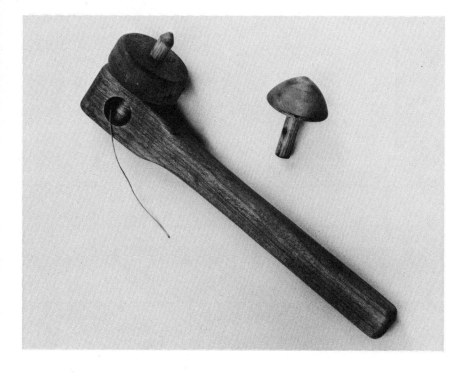

The secret to a long-spinning top is symmetry—it's got to be balanced. Never mind the geometric formula, simply drill the hole for the spindle in the exact center of the top body. Glue in the spindle and mount it in the drill chuck. Spinning the top in the drill, sand the body until it is perfectly round and balanced. Then sand a point on the lower end of the spindle.

The yoke cradles the top so you can really yank the string.

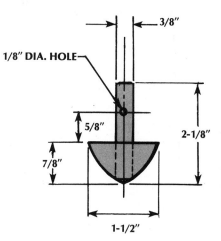

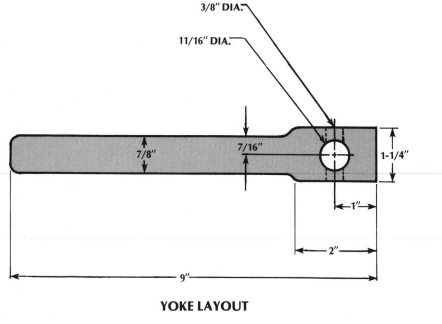

YOKE LAYOUT

TOP LAYOUTS

From *HANDS ON* May/June 82

Get the children in your life hooked on woodworking early. Let them use this custom-made mallet as much as they want on their own pounding bench!

Start this child's toy with a hardwood stock such as poplar, maple, or birch.

Begin by cutting the bench and ends to size. Cut the dado in the ends that will accept the top. Lay out and cut the profile on the ends.

Lay out and drill the 1" diameter peg holes in the bench. Dry-assemble and clamp the bench together and round all edges.

Turn the pegs three at a time allowing extra stock for the lathe centers. Cut the pegs to length and chamfer the ends.

Tilt the bandsaw table 45° to form a V-block, and using the miter gauge as a fence, cut the relief slots in each end of the pegs.

Turn the mallet head and handle. If you wish to turn the handle elliptically, turn the handle round, then offset one end 1/4" in two directions.

Finish sand all pieces. Stain each piece with food coloring mixed with water (two parts food coloring to one part water). Glue top and end together, then seal with a nontoxic finish.

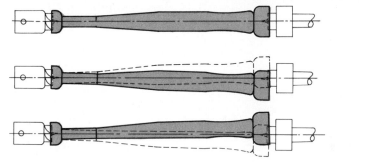

Turning the mallet handle.

3/4" DIA. HOLE

D

E

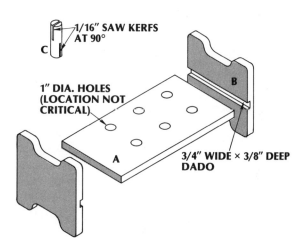

1/16" SAW KERFS AT 90°

C

B

1" DIA. HOLES (LOCATION NOT CRITICAL)

A

3/4" WIDE × 3/8" DEEP DADO

LIST OF MATERIALS

(finished dimensions in inches)

A	Top	3/4 × 8 × 15
B	End (2)	3/4 × 8 × 8
C	Peg	1 dia. × 3-1/2
D	Head	1-5/8 dia. × 3-3/8
E	Handle	3/4 × 1 × 9

From *HANDS ON* Nov/Dec 79

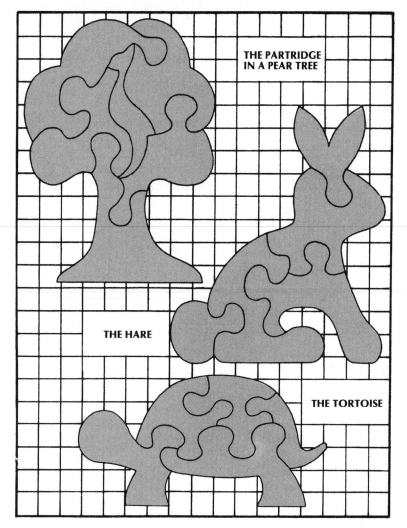

THE PARTRIDGE IN A PEAR TREE

THE HARE

THE TORTOISE

Puzzles have always been popular with children and are one of the few toys that come apart without breaking. The puzzles we have included here have one added attraction—they stand up on their own when a child pieces them together.

1. Glue up stock 1-1/2" thick or thicker. If you're making the Tortoise, your stock needs to be 6" × 11-1/2"; the Hare, 10" × 11-1/4"; the Partridge in a Pear Tree, 8-3/4" × 11-1/2". When making the partridge, consider using a contrasting color of wood. We have made a walnut partridge to roost in a poplar pear tree.

2. Cut out the contour of the puzzle.

3. Using a saw with a thin blade, cut out the separate pieces of the puzzle. A bandsaw with a 3/16" or 1/8" blade works well; so does a coping saw or sabre saw with a scroll blade. If you use a jigsaw, use soft wood and a slow speed. Otherwise, the blade will warp in the wood and the pieces of the puzzle will not slide together smoothly.

Using our puzzles as examples, you can design your own around your child's favorite animal or object. When cutting the pieces, take care that you use enough reverse curves, or heads and necks, so that they all interlock.

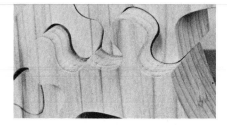

Each piece of a stand-up puzzle should interlock with the adjoining pieces.

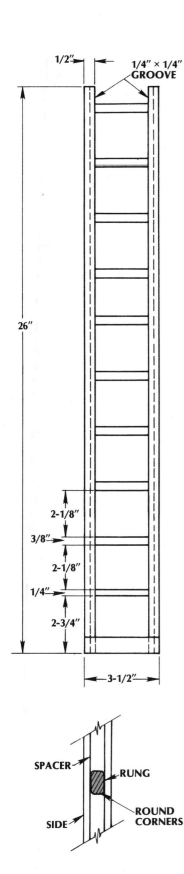

Young and old alike are amused by this clever toy. The bottom rung of the ladder is the trick that keeps the firemen on the ladder at the bottom.

1. Cut all pieces for the ladder and base. Precision is important. Plans show a 1/4″ × 1/4″ groove to accept rungs and spacers. You can make this with the table saw and dado accessory. An alternative method is to form the ladder by using a 1/4″ mortising attachment to form squared holes for each of the rungs.

2. Assemble all parts using woodworker's glue. Then round all sharp edges. Too large a flat on rungs (D) will slow or stop the action of the toy.

3. Make the racers (F) following the pattern provided. Drill the holes in each racer; then, cut them on the bandsaw or jigsaw. Sand and fit them to the ladder. Apply a nontoxic finish. A little paraffin helps to lubricate the racers on their journey; furthermore, you may choose to make them of hardwood.

LIST OF MATERIALS

(finished dimensions in inches)

A	Base	3/4 × 3-1/2 × 5
B	Sides (2)	1/2 × 3/4 × 26
C	Spacers (20)	1/4 × 1/4 × 2-1/8
D	Rungs (9)	1/4 × 3/8 × 3
E	Rung	1/4 dia. × 3
F	Racers (2)	3/4 × 1 × 2-1/2

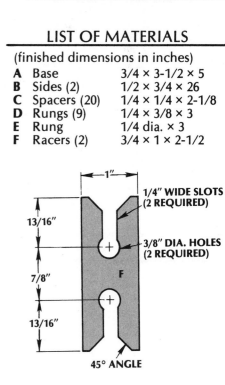

KITE STRING WINDER

From *HANDS ON* Mar/Apr 81

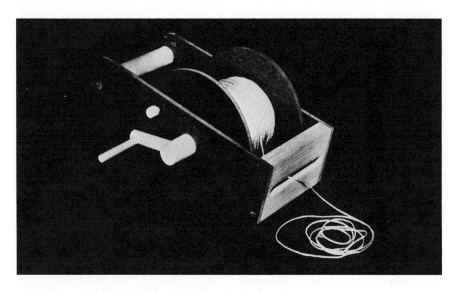

Look up in the sky on a blustery spring afternoon and you're likely to find it dotted with kites. And down on the ground, plenty of kids struggling with the kite strings. Here's a simple kite string winder that takes the frustration out of kite flying.

Turn a large dowel on the lathe 3-1/2″ in diameter. Cut this into a 3-1/2″ long section and make this section into a spool by gluing a washer (D) on each end. Drill a 1″ hole through the center of the spool.

Assemble winder frame with the handle (E) at one end and the string feeder (A) at the other. This feeder has a slot routed in it to help feed the string onto the spool evenly.

Make the crank (G, H) and axle (F) out of dowel stock. Pass the axle through the side (B) with the spool (C) in place and fix the spool to the axle with a dowel. Wooden or hardboard washers (D) will keep the spool from rubbing on the sides (B).

Drill one of the sides for a locking pin (J). If you wish, this pin can be attached to the frame with string to prevent youngsters from losing it.

LIST OF MATERIALS

(finished dimensions in inches)

A	String feeder	3/4 × 3 × 4-1/2
B	Sides (2)	1/4 × 3 × 11
C	Spool	3-1/2 dia. × 3-1/2
D	Washers	2 dia. × 1/4
E	Handle	1 dia. × 4-1/2
F	Axle	1 dia. × 6-3/8
G	Crank handle support	3/8 dia. × 3-1/2
H	Crank handle	3/8 dia. × 2-5/8
J	Locking pin	1/4 (I.D.) × 1/2 (O.D.) × 1-1/4
K	#6 × 3/4 Flathead wood screws (6)	
L	1″ I.D. Washers (2)	

CROSS SECTION OF PART A

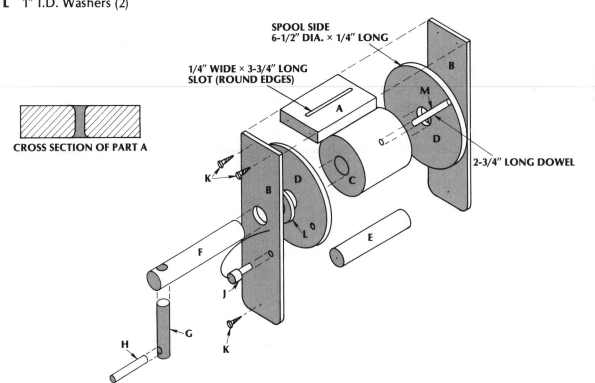

SPOOL SIDE
6-1/2″ DIA. × 1/4″ LONG

1/4″ WIDE × 3-3/4″ LONG
SLOT (ROUND EDGES)

2-3/4″ LONG DOWEL

Delight the toddler in your life with this cute little puppy. He loves to chase and nip at the heels of children who squeal with joy. Here's how to make it.

Transfer the pattern to 1/2" stock. Note that there are three pieces and they overlap at the finger joints. Cut out the dog body on the band-saw or Jigsaw. Next, put the pieces together and drill a 1/8" hole for the 1/8" dowel hinge pin. Sand the body of the dog, rounding off all edges, and round the joints. Glue the hinge pins in place. Cut the 3/4" × 3/4" × 3-1/4" wheel holders and form the 1/2" wide × 3/8" deep dadoes in them. Glue and clamp the dog body to the axle holders. After the glue has dried, clamp the dog to the worktable and use the horizontal boring mode to drill the 5/16" axle holes. You can make your own wheels with a hole saw, turn them on the lathe, or buy wheels at a craft store. Attach them to the axle with glue. Paint the dog with nontoxic paints. Cut ears out of vinyl or leather and attach with glue. Finally, mount a screw eye in the front for the pull string.

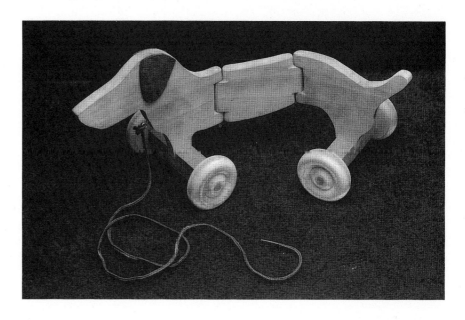

ONE SQUARE = 1/2"

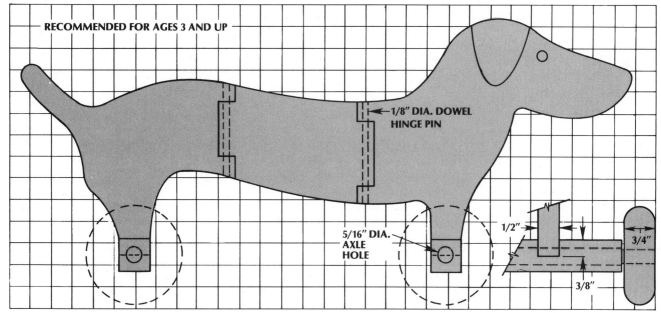

RECOMMENDED FOR AGES 3 AND UP

1/8" DIA. DOWEL HINGE PIN

5/16" DIA. AXLE HOLE

1/2"

3/4"

3/8"

Index

Many thanks to the following *HANDS ON* readers who contributed to this book:
DANIEL AGUIAR, JEAN BUTLER, DOUG ELLIS, JACK FISHER, JIMMIE FREEMAN,
KENNY GREINER, VAL HAFNER, ROGER HAVERLOCK, GARY HAVERMAN,
DAVID HEMBERGER, RICHARD HOLMES, ROBERT LEE, DORIS K. LORENZ,
W. C. MADDEN, ROBERT MILLER, GILBERT OLSEN, LARRY PEABODY, ED PETERSON,
DALE ROESCH, PHIL ROSILE, JOHN TRAUB, BASIL WENTWORTH,
KENNETH YEARWOOD, and VERNON YOUNG.